STRIVING LESS
AND TRUSTING
GOD MORE

Isaiah

FOR TEEN GIRLS

MELISSA
SPOELSTRA

Lifeway Press®
Nashville, Tennessee

Published by Lifeway Press® • © 2022 Melissa Spoelstra

No part of this book may be reproduced or transmitted in any form or by any means, electronic or mechanical, including photocopying and recording, or by any information storage or retrieval system, except as may be expressly permitted in writing by the publisher. Requests for permission should be addressed in writing to Lifeway Press˚; 200 Powell Place, Suite 100; Brentwood, TN 37027.

ISBN: 978-1-0877-6230-2 • Item: 005837087
Dewey decimal classification: 224.1
Subject headings: TRUST / BIBLE. O.T. ISAIAH—STUDY AND TEACHING / GOD—WILL

Unless indicated otherwise, all Scripture quotations are taken from the Holy Bible, New Living Translation, copyright ©1996, 2004, 2007, 2013, 2015 by Tyndale House Foundation. Used by permission of Tyndale House Publishers, Inc., Carol Stream, IL 60188. All rights reserved. Scripture marked ESV is taken from The ESV® Bible (The Holy Bible, English Standard Version®) copyright © 2001 by Crossway, a publishing ministry of Good News Publishers. ESV® Text Edition: 2011. All rights reserved. Scripture marked NIV is taken from the THE HOLY BIBLE, NEW INTERNATIONAL VERSION®, NIV® Copyright © 1973, 1978, 1984 by Biblica, Inc.® Used by permission. All rights reserved worldwide. Scripture marked CSB is taken from the Christian Standard Bible®, Copyright © 2017 by Holman Bible Publishers. Used by permission. Christian Standard Bible® and CSB® are federally registered trademarks of Holman Bible Publishers. Scripture marked NASB are taken from the New American Standard Bible® (NASB), Copyright © 1960, 1962, 1963, 1968, 1971, 1972, 1973, 1975, 1977, 1995 by The Lockman Foundation. Used by permission. www.lockman.org. Scripture marked NKJV are taken from the New King James Version®. Copyright © 1982 by Thomas Nelson. Used by permission. All rights reserved.

To order additional copies of this resource, write to Lifeway Resources Customer Service; 200 Powell Place, Suite 100; Brentwood, TN 37027; order online at www.lifeway.com; fax 615.251.5933; phone toll free 800.458.2772; or email orderentry@lifeway.com.

Printed in the United States of America

Lifeway Girls Bible Studies • Lifeway Resources
• 200 Powell Place, Suite 100 • Brentwood, TN 37027

Cover design by Shiloh Stufflebeam

Contents

About the Author

Melissa Spoelstra is a women's conference speaker, Bible teacher, and author who is madly in love with Jesus. She is passionate about studying God's Word and helping women of all ages to seek Christ and know Him more intimately through serious Bible study. Melissa has a degree in Bible theology, and she enjoys teaching God's Word to the body of Christ, traveling to diverse groups and churches across the nation.

Melissa is the author of many Bible studies, including *Acts: Awakening to God in Everyday Life* and *The Names of God: His Character Revealed*. She has also authored several books, including *Dare to Hope* and *Total Family Makeover: 8 Practical Steps to Making Disciples at Home*. She is a regular contributor to the Proverbs 31 First Five App, the *Girlfriends in God* online daily devotional, and many magazines and blogs. Melissa enjoys spending time with her pastor husband, Sean, and their four adult children: Zach, Abby, Sara, and Rachel.

DEDICATION

This Bible study is dedicated to my three daughters:

Abby
Sarah
Rachel

I'm so grateful to have walked alongside you during your teen years. Through the joys and struggles, I watched you rumble with your faith, and it brings my heart great joy to watch each of you striving less and trusting God more as young women. Keep your eyes on our faithful God who longs to renew your strength and uphold you with His righteous right hand.

FOLLOW MELISSA

Twitter	@MelSpoelstra
Instagram	@Melissa.Spoelstra
Facebook	/AuthorMelissaSpoelstra
Website	MelissaSpoelstra.com

INTRODUCING
Isaiah

I wonder if you've ever left a church service, girl's conference, or Bible study determined to do better. Maybe you promised yourself you'd pray regularly, show more kindness to others, or be a better person in general. This determination usually comes from a desire to grow spiritually and know God better. But where has this intense pursuit of changing our behaviors gotten us? How's that "striving" been working out for you?

I can tell you how it has worked for me. My attempts at heart transformation have left me with guilt and frustration, and they have caused me to go backward rather than forward in intimacy with God. When I've succeeded in the short term, I've often become prideful. Then in moments of failure, I've experienced shame. God doesn't want either of these postures for us.

Wanting spiritual change in our lives isn't a bad thing, we just have to guard against relying on our own effort to bring it about. As we set out together to study the prophet Isaiah's biblical book, we will discover a simple but life-changing truth: *Following God isn't about striving; it's about trusting God more.* The prophet Isaiah served as God's mouthpiece to the people of God and the surrounding nations. And his message reverberates through our lives today as we read Isaiah's call to rely on the Lord.

Using the genres of poetry, narrative, and prophecy, Isaiah teaches that followers of God can trust His:

- Character
- Calendar
- Comfort

- Commands
- Correction
- Coming Again

That all sounds so good! But I know by now that there are times when I say, "I trust God," but my stress, worry, and lack of peace don't point to that kind of faith. Trust can be complicated, especially when people in our lives have broken it. Maybe someone you counted on for protection and provision let you down. Maybe you invested your time and energy into a group at church but felt betrayed or overlooked. It can be easy to transfer our trust issues from relationships with people onto our relationship with God.

Then there are other times when we thought we put our trust in God, but what we expected Him to do didn't happen. He may have been working behind the scenes, but we couldn't see how at the time. When He doesn't do what we want Him to do, we can inch our way toward self-sufficiency (relying on ourselves) without even realizing it.

Isaiah was human just like us, and yet he radically trusted God and called anyone who would listen to do the same. His message highlights freedom from captivity and light breaking through darkness for those who would heed his words. Anyone in need of a little freedom and light in their thoughts, attitudes, or actions? Unpacking Isaiah's words will reveal that we can trust God more than our own human effort or the counterfeits the world suggests.

Isaiah has been referred to as "a Bible in miniature."[1] The book's sixty-six chapters and the Bible's sixty-six books include all genres of biblical literature, such as historical narrative, poetry, and prophecy. Some have compared Isaiah's first thirty-nine chapters with the thirty-nine books of the Old Testament because of the emphasis on God's judgment toward sin, while the last twenty-seven chapters parallel the New Testament's focus on God's grace.[2]

Isaiah has also been referred to as the fifth Gospel because of the number of Messianic references found in the book. Isaiah's words are quoted in the New Testament more times than any other Old Testament book.

Isaiah wrote messages of both judgment and hope. Pastor H. B. Charles wrote, "Real faith is ambidextrous. It can take blessings in one hand and trouble in the other, lifting both in the worship of the God who is worthy of our stubborn trust, complete obedience, and unceasing praise."[3] Throughout our study of Isaiah, we'll learn to be ambidextrous. Hopefully by the time we turn the last page, we will be able to lift both hands in worship. We won't be striving harder but instead trusting more deeply the Faithful One who is so worthy of our complete dependence.

A FINAL WORD

I can't wait to get started on this journey alongside you. I don't want us to keep striving and falling into a cycle of guilt when it comes to our faith. Instead, we can pursue God's heart and seek to trust Him more. Out of that trust, I believe we will find comfort and peace to sustain us as we hold trouble in one hand and blessing in another. I'm praying that you will join me as we let go of striving and answer Isaiah's call to the trust the Lord!

Melissa

HOW TO USE THIS STUDY

In our time together, we'll be looking at Scripture through a dual lens of history and modern day. Simply put, we'll seek to understand what Isaiah's prophetic words would've meant to his original audience, the Israelites, as well as how they apply to our lives today. Through poetry, narrative, and prophecy, we'll see themes of judgment and hope displayed—leading to our ultimate hope, Jesus. As Isaiah varied the presentation of His message, we'll vary our study too. Here's what that'll look like:

PERSONAL BIBLE STUDY   GROUP TIME   WATCH

The "Personal Bible Study" is for you to work through the Scripture on your own. Feel free to complete each between our weekly group times as you see fit throughout the week. The "Group Time" and "Watch" sections are meant to be completed with your small group.

PERSONAL BIBLE STUDY

You'll kick off each week with five days of personal Bible study—written to help structure your personal time with the Lord, deepen your understanding of a Big Idea, and move you to trust God more.

Each day includes:

- Scripture passage(s) to study, consider, and memorize
- Questions to help you examine the Scripture and apply it

And for Day Five of each session of our study, we'll look at the session's theme through a Messianic lens focusing on Jesus in Isaiah. I know it can be tempting to skip days of personal study here and there, especially as you get to the end of a week, but I want to encourage you to press on because of the treasure you'll find in studying Christ during the last study of each week.

It's okay if you're still struggling with the Big Idea when you finish your personal study. The goal isn't to understand God completely; it's to trust Him fully, even when we don't understand.

GROUP TIME

I hope you have an awesome group of girls who are doing this study alongside you. It makes Bible study way more fun and a little less intimidating when you're not doing it alone. Session 1 will be your first group time together and will give you all the opportunity to see what this study is all about. After each week of personal study, you will have a chance to reflect and discuss as a group. However, for the first week, there's no personal study so you'll view the intro video and discuss the overview of Isaiah.

As you watch each video, I encourage you to take notes using the fill-in-the-blanks and notes box to keep track of anything you don't want to forget!

If you're a leader, make sure you check out the leader guide in the back of the book on page 166 for more tips on how to make the most of the time with your group.

RESOURCES

We've also added some awesome resources in the back of this book to help you deepen your study of the book of Isaiah:

- USE THE MOM & DAUGHTER GUIDE on pages 168-169 if you want to walk through what you're learning with your mom or a godly woman in your life.

- USE THE CHECKLIST on page 170 to read the entire book of Isaiah during or after your study.

- IF YOU HAVE QUESTIONS ABOUT BECOMING A CHRISTIAN or sharing the gospel with a friend, check out How to Become a Christian on page 171.

Session One

GROUP TIME

DISCUSS
Discuss the following questions as you kick off this Bible study with your group.

Recall some things you already knew about the book of Isaiah.

Share about a time when you left a church service, Bible study, girls conference, or youth camp determined to "do better." How were you striving to do better?

How can we help one another guard against relying on our own effort for spiritual change?

Name the six ways Isaiah said we can trust the Lord. (See page 6 for help.)

What things in our lives might point to a lack of faith even when we say, "I trust God"?

List some ways people in our lives might break our trust. How could these affect our willingness to trust God?

Describe some feelings people tend to have about the word *judgment*. What are some ways we can help others see how hope and judgment work together?

MEMORIZE
Go ahead and read next week's memory verse, Isaiah 1:18, aloud together.

WATCH

Use the fill-in-the-blanks and note-taking space as you watch the Session 1 teaching video together as a group.

Hope and judgment are not a _____ to be solved, but a _____ to be embraced.

_____ _____ truth is what will help us navigate _____ _____ times.

We need to let God be _____ so that we can be _____.

We need to realign to God's _____ so that we can trust His _____.

Where we look for _____ will either weaken or strengthen us spiritually.

What's in our _____ will end up in our _____.

He loves us too much to leave us on the path to _____.

We're going to see how we can live in the light of _____ _____.

In the first thirty-nine chapters, it seems like God is _____ the comfortable while in the last twenty-seven chapters, God is _____ the afflicted.

NOTES

PRAY

Father, please guide us as we begin the journey of learning how to strive less and trust You more.

TRUST *God's* CHARACTER

SESSION TWO

We can't trust someone unless we know that person has our best interests in mind. When it comes to the Lord, you may know He loves you, but have you ever wondered why He isn't fixing something you really want to be fixed? This week, we'll explore God's character. Isaiah reveals the Lord as holy, as the one we should revere as Almighty. Isaiah also tells us our God is forgiving and merciful—He transforms our sins until they are white as snow.

I'm so glad you're joining me on this journey into deeper trust. As we take a fresh look at Isaiah's message in light of God's attributes, we'll understand that our Redeemer is passionately committed to us. We don't want our relationship with Him to be about changing our behaviors temporarily; rather, we want to allow the Holy One of Israel to do real transforming work in our hearts. This won't be accomplished by swatting at our bad habits but by growing a bigger view of our God who longs for us to strive less and trust Him more.

MEMORY VERSE

"Come now, let's settle this," says the LORD. "Though your sins are like scarlet, I will make them as white as snow. Though they are red like crimson, I will make them as white as wool."

ISAIAH 1:18

BIG IDEA

We can trust
God because
He is passionately
committed to us.

Day One

PASSIONATE COMMITMENT

I noticed a huge streak of blue on one of my favorite shirts as I pulled it from the dryer. The entire load had similar marks, and I found a blue ink pen fully emptied of its contents. I had heard hairspray could remove ink, so I sprayed, rubbed, and rinsed until the fumes were more than I could handle. Finally, I surrendered to the permanence of the stains and threw out the entire load. While the loss of those clothes frustrated me, I wasn't passionately committed to them. I tried to make them clean, but I couldn't.

At times in my life, I've felt like that stained laundry and wondered if I'm worth God's effort during all my struggles and failures. Can you relate? Thankfully, our God doesn't treat us as replaceable. I hope today we can put those nagging thoughts behind us as we discover just how passionately committed the Lord is to His people.

Isaiah was written more than twenty-seven hundred years ago by a man who obeyed God's call to be His prophet, God's mouthpiece to His people. Isaiah spoke to his original audience regarding current events and prophesied happenings that have since been fulfilled—like the birth of the Messiah—and some that have yet to come to fruition as they speak of the future return of Christ. As we move through this study, we'll first look at Isaiah's intent for the initial recipients of his words and then the biblical principles that apply in our lives today.

SINS LIKE SCARLET

Isaiah's name means, *"Yahweh is salvation."*[1]

READ ISAIAH 1:1. What did you learn about Isaiah from the introduction to his book?

While we want to get to know Isaiah, we'll need to be patient as his first vision tells us more about his people, the Judeans, than it tells us about him.

NOW READ ISAIAH 1:2-5. Name at least three things you learn about the character of God's people at the time of Isaiah's writing.

-
-
-

READ ISAIAH 1:6-9. Summarize in a sentence the circumstances God's people faced at the time of Isaiah's vision.

Sin brought suffering into the lives of God's people. Let's be clear: not all of our problems are rooted in personal sin, but we would not have any problems if sin didn't exist. We have to be careful not to assign specific causes and effects to our trials, but we often can draw a connection between sin and suffering. God's people reaped what they had sown, and the Lord didn't leave them guessing about what had Him so upset.

READ ISAIAH 1:10-15. List some of the verbs God used to describe His reaction to their actions.

When God reacts this strongly to His beloved people, we should pay attention so we can know what hurts His heart. These were some of the complaints He lodged against Isaiah's people: they made sacrifices out of routine instead of repentance or obedience to God; they gave meaningless gifts and offerings; they celebrated, fasted, and attended religious meetings for outward show; and they prayed to God while preying on the innocent.

How would you sum up this behavior in one or two words?

Isaiah 1:4-17 uses the literary genre of an extended poem consisting of four elements: "a general indictment (v. 4), a lament about Israel's true and pitiful situation (vv. 5-9), a refusal to heed Israel in time of need (vv. 10-15), and a summons to reformation (vv. 16-17)."[2]

The word *hypocrisy* came to mind as I read these verses. It wasn't the *use* but the *abuse* of spiritual practices that brought such a strong reaction from God. The people were going through the motions of spiritual worship without a personal connection to the Lord and His laws. God called out the contradiction in their lives of uniting spiritual practices with unrepentant sin. God invites His people into a relationship, expecting repentance and obedience to follow.

Before we condemn the rebellious people in these pages, let's bring Isaiah's words a little closer to home. I can relate to projecting a spiritual image on the outside while struggling to live those truths or failing to grow my relationship with God—especially when no one is looking.

Reflect on any spiritual inconsistency in your life (thoughts, judgments, attitudes, actions). How have the truths we've read so far in Isaiah convicted you?

WHITE AS SNOW

The assurance of forgiveness for those who repent is continually confirmed throughout the book of Isaiah (12:1; 30:18-19; 33:24; 38:17; 40:1-2; 43:25; 44:22; 59:20) pointing ultimately to Christ's sacrifice—prophesied as the Suffering Servant in Isaiah 52:13–53:12.[4]

READ ISAIAH 1:16-17. What hope do you see for the nation of Judah? What were some changes God required to restore their relationship to Him?

No matter how far we've sunk in our sin, God remains committed to us, and He invites us to turn from our sin and turn toward Him. Only with repentant hearts are we able to live as the people God created us to be—those who love Him and love others.

The "scarlet" or "crimson" mentioned in Isaiah 1:18 referenced a dye made from an insect that permanently marked garments.[3] The hearers would have understood it to be something like the ink stains in my laundry. As Christ followers today, we see in this verse a picture of Jesus's work on our behalf. Through the blood of Christ—not any amount of human scrubbing—the stain of our sin can be removed permanently.

LOVED AND FORGIVEN

Throughout the pages of Isaiah, we'll find God encouraging His people that forgiveness is available. His plan to send Jesus was already in motion—the people of Isaiah's day could believe faithfully that a Messiah would come. In the same way, we can rely on the truth that Jesus makes our scarlet sins "as white as snow" (v. 18). You can trust God's character because He is passionately committed to His people. His plan is for your cleansing and renewal. The Lord hates sin because of its destructive power, but He loves and is committed to redeeming sinners!

And let's settle this right at the beginning of our study: You can't out-sin God's grace. Lies the enemy may be using against you are just NOT true. Not the lie that you're just too much to handle; or you will never be able to change; or your sins are worse than other people's sins; or that the stain of your mistakes will always follow you. Your God is passionately committed to you!

Take a moment to feel the full weight of God's passion and forgiveness for you. Write your name in the blank:

"Come now, let's settle this," says the LORD.
"Though [_____'s] sins are like scarlet,
I will make them as white as snow.
Though they are red like crimson,
I will make them as white as wool."
ISAIAH 1:18

Even if it feels like your life has been through the spin cycle followed by heat that set the stains of your past, you can become white as snow because the God you serve is passionately committed to you.

DAILY WRAP-UP

Today we focused on this truth: *We can trust God because He is passionately committed to us.* **How would you summarize your personal takeaway from today's study?**

PRAYER

Lord, thank You for Your passion and commitment to me. Most days I don't feel white like snow. I battle against the problems in life and my own sin on a regular basis. Help me to strive less and trust more. I'm so glad You don't require me to earn my way to You through religious works and instead invite me into a personal relationship. Remind me of this truth often because I'm so prone to forget it! In Jesus's name, amen.

MEMORY VERSE ACTIVITY

Read Isaiah 1:18 aloud three times. You can find it printed on this page.

Day Two

HOLY AND HIGHER

BIG IDEA
We can trust
God because
He is holy.

Parents might use a chore chart at home to teach responsibility and consequences. But these things are never about our status in the family We do work because we're part of the family—not to earn our place in it. But sometimes we still bring a "working to earn my place in the family" mentality into our relationship with the Lord.

As we dig into Isaiah 6 today, we find a progression of belief, which leads to a sense of belonging, which then results in transformed behavior. The order of this progression is important:

One distinction of Isaiah's writing is his use of the name for God as the "Holy One of Israel." While it is found thirty-one times in the Old Testament, no fewer than twenty-five are found in Isaiah.[6]

SEEING THE LORD (6:1-4)   →   BELIEF

SEEING OURSELVES (6:5-7)   →   BELONGING BECAUSE GOD CLEANSES OUR SIN

SEEING OUR NEXT STEPS (6:8)   →   BEHAVIOR

For clarity in decisions, we must to focus on the Lord—and ourselves in relation to Him—so we can have a proper perspective to receive direction.

SEEING THE LORD

When words are repeated twice in Scripture, it indicates superiority. Repeating a word three times shows that this is the ultimate/highest point of that feature. Isaiah used "holy, holy, holy" to mean God is absolutely, perfectly holy. He is holier than everyone and everything else.

READ ISAIAH 6:1-4. Either sketch or write a short description of the scene Isaiah encountered.

Visualize this scene: The ultimate authority of heaven and earth sits on His throne wearing a robe that fills the temple. He is attended by angels called seraphim who call out to each other, "Holy, holy, holy" (v. 3). This is the only biblical passage where heavenly beings are called "seraphim." "The seraphs are bright creatures, for the word means 'burning ones'; yet they hide their faces from the greater brightness and glory of the Lord."[7] Their words shake the room and smoke fills the entire temple.

Jot down a few words to describe how you would've reacted if you were Isaiah and actually witnessed this with your own eyes.

I think I would have been overcome with the holiness or "otherness" of it all. No movie, novel, or dream could compare with a glimpse of the living God. While God forgives and loves us as sinners, desiring a relationship with us, we should not be tempted to bring Him down to our human level. These verses remind us that He is holy. The Hebrew for holy is *qadowsh,* which means "sacred, holy, Holy One, saint, set apart."[7] To say God is holy means He is set apart. He is not like us. He is perfect in all He does. He rules supremely and receives the worship of an array of heavenly beings.

Write a few sentences praising God as the Holy One you worship today.

SEEING OURSELVES

READ ISAIAH 6:5-7. Summarize Isaiah's response and the angel's actions in your own words.

ISAIAH'S RESPONSE	ANGEL'S ACTIONS

In response to God's holiness, Isaiah recognized his own sinfulness. He didn't try to hide or pretend; instead, he confessed his predicament. Once we see the Lord, we can then gain clarity about our own position in relation to Him. Let's take a moment to join Isaiah today.

Tell the Lord in a few sentences how you feel about your own sinfulness in light of His holiness.

Confession as a spiritual practice should lead us toward God rather than away from Him. I love that the Lord didn't shame Isaiah in his brokenness but removed his guilt. The imagery of the burning coal taken from the altar reminds us that the Lord longs to cleanse us as well. Jesus offered His life as payment for our sins. His altar was a cross where He removed our guilt and forgave our sins through His shed blood.

Every Gospel references the words from Isaiah 6:9-10 in connection with the parable of the sower (Matt. 13:14-15; Mark 4:10-12; Luke 8:10; John 12:39-41), and the last verse in chapter 6 speaks of Israel's stump becoming a holy seed.

SEEING OUR NEXT STEPS

READ ISAIAH 6:8-13. What did the Lord ask, and how did Isaiah respond (v. 8)?

What is your initial reaction to the message the Lord gave Isaiah (vv. 9-13)?

First, Isaiah saw the Lord (Isa. 6:1-4); then, he saw himself clearly (Isa. 6:5-7). Only then did he receive the call to prophesy (Isa. 6:8). The message the Lord gave him to share wasn't the touchy-feely inspiration I was expecting. The Lord knew His own people would reject Him for many generations and reap the consequences of their choices. Verses like these give us an opportunity to trust that God knows and sees more than we do.

God's instructions aren't always what we're expecting. In Isaiah's eagerness to answer God's call, it's hard to believe he knew the difficult task that awaited him and the challenging words God would ask him to deliver. The moments when life doesn't go as we think it should provide the clearest opportunities to exercise trust in our relationship with Him. Sometimes the only next step we can take to say to God, "Here I am."

Reflect on a time when what was happening in your life didn't match up with what you thought the Lord should be doing. What was your main question for God then?

Maybe you've experienced something completely devastating, and when the Lord didn't intervene, you began to lose trust in Him. These are the moments when we need reminders of His character so that we can press into our faith.

READ ISAIAH 55:8-9 and underline the words <u>thoughts</u> and <u>ways</u>:

"My thoughts are nothing like your thoughts," says the LORD.
"And my ways are far beyond anything you could imagine.
For just as the heavens are higher than the earth,
so my ways are higher than your ways
and my thoughts higher than your thoughts."

Think about something in your past from the perspective that God's thoughts and ways were higher than yours. How might this change your perspective?

You may not always understand what God is doing in the moment, but you can always trust Him! He knows you don't always follow all His instructions, and thankfully, you don't have to earn your way into His family. If you have believed in Him by faith, then you belong to Him. He loves you and knows better than you do what is best for your life because His thoughts and ways are higher than yours.

DAILY WRAP-UP

Today we focused on this truth: *We can trust God because He is holy.* How would you summarize your personal takeaway from today's study?

BIG IDEA

We can trust God
because He makes
Himself known.

Day Three

POWER IN THE NAME

Who has earned your trust over time? Why?

Trust grows as we realize someone is safe and has our best interests
at heart. One of the best ways for us to trust God and understand His
character is by examining some of His names revealed in His Word.

READ ISAIAH 45. Record God's names along with any
thoughts, insights, or comments regarding each name in
the chart below.

VERSE	NAME/ DESCRIPTION OF GOD	OPTIONAL COMMENTS
1	LORD	LORD in all caps refers to Yahweh in the Bible.
3	God of Israel	He calls us by name.
9		
11		
13		
14		
15		

Highlight the name that stands out most to you.

Maybe you were surprised by how many different names you found. But God's greatness can't be summarized in just one. These expressions are just the tip of the iceberg in the book of Isaiah. Eighteen times throughout his book, Isaiah referred to God as the "Sovereign LORD" (NLT)—and thirty times as "Lord GOD" in the CSB)—which is *Adonai Yahweh* in Hebrew. *Redeemer* is used in thirteen instances with other mentions like *Immanuel, the First and the Last,* our *Judge, Shepherd, Warrior, Rock, Mighty One,* and *Everlasting God.* These grow our knowledge of God's character.

Yahweh comes from the Hebrew tetragram made up by the four-letters YHWH and was considered so holy that even scribes didn't say it out loud. Later, vowels from the name Adonai were added to form the name Yahweh. Scholars in the Middle Ages were the first to translate Yahweh with the English rendering Jehovah.[9]

Now we'll focus on just four names we discovered in Isaiah 45 and see how they can help us know and trust God more: *Yahweh, Elohim, Creator,* and *Savior.* Then, we'll write a trust statement related to each name.

YAHWEH

Yahweh is translated using capital letters—LORD—to distinguish it from *Adonai* which most Bibles render "Lord" in lowercase. *Yahweh* is the personal name God used when talking to Moses at the burning bush, and God described it as "my eternal name, my name to remember for all generations" (Ex. 3:15). Most scholars associate YHWH with the verb "to be," so this name is sometimes defined as "the self-existent One."[8] Yahweh has always been and continues to be completely self-sustaining and self-sufficient.

Take a moment now to fill in the blanks as you think about Yahweh and the concerns or blessings in your life:

I can trust Yahweh with _____

because He is _____.

ELOHIM

When you recorded *God* on your chart, the original Hebrew was either *El* or *Elohim.* (It varied in Isaiah 45. *Elohim* is actually a plural form of *El.*) *Elohim* is used more than two thousand times in the Old Testament, making it the word used to identify God most often in Scripture.[10] While the original audience wouldn't have understood the plural name as referring to the Trinity, we know God is Father, Son, and Holy Spirit because He has revealed Himself over time.

Scripture tells us our God is transcendent, creative, and powerful. At times I try to reduce God to something I can understand and define, but we can't put *Elohim* in a box. He exists outside of time. He made the beginning and already knows the end. This stretches my brain to its edges because I live by a calendar and a clock.

Fill in this blank: I can trust Elohim today because He is a God who

_____

_____.

CREATOR

Isaiah 45:9 referenced God as *Maker* or *Creator*. The Hebrew word is *Yatsar*, which means "to form, fashion, frame."[11] Isaiah used the illustration of the potter and his clay to help the people understand God's authority to shape us according to His design. Over the course of our study, we will also find three mentions of God as the Potter and His people as clay (29:16; 41:25; 64:8).

Isaiah's original audience argued against God's instructions, but Isaiah reminded them of God's position. When we see God as our Maker, we learn to trust Him even through painful processes of shaping, cutting away, and then firing to solidify us according His design. As we consider God as former, fashioner, and framer in our lives, we can loosen our grip on our illusion of control and concentrate on being moldable clay in His hands.

Fill in this blank: Creator God, soften and mold me when it comes to

_____

_____.

SAVIOR

While God is *Yahweh* (self-existent), *Elohim* (our God), *Creator* (with complete authority to mold and shape us), may we never lose sight that He is also *Savior,* the One who longs to save us. In Isaiah 45, both verses 15 and 21 used *Savior* to describe our God. Jesus reminded us of God's desire to save us. Just after He declared that God loved the world and gave His Son so that those who believe in Him "will not perish but have eternal life" (John 3:16), Jesus said this: "God sent his Son into the world not to judge the world, but to save the world through him" (John 3:17).

Both Isaiah's name in Hebrew and Jesus's name in Greek mean "Yahweh is salvation." We never want to forget God's power and authority, but we also don't want to lose sight of His goodness to deliver us from sin.

Fill in these blanks for our final name today:

I can trust God to rescue me from _____

_____

because His name means _____.

We just scratched the surface with four names found in Isaiah today. Which one of the names we focused on most resonated you? Why?

I'm so thankful that we serve a God who invites us to draw near (Jas. 4:8). Just as it takes time to develop trust in human relationships, our trust in the Lord grows as we pursue a deeper walk with Him.

DAILY WRAP-UP

Today we focused on this truth: *We can trust God because He makes Himself known.* How would you summarize your personal takeaway from today's study?

PRAYER

Yahweh, You are the great I AM! Elohim, Your power and might is beyond all I can think or imagine. Creator, You have the authority to shape and fashion my life according to Your design even when it doesn't make sense to me. Soften me under Your gentle hands. Savior, I'm so grateful You believe I'm worth rescuing. God, continue to reveal Yourself to me as I study Your words of truth. In Jesus's name, amen.

MEMORY VERSE ACTIVITY

Write down Isaiah 1:18. Also record one thought you have as you read over this verse.

BIG IDEA
We can trust God
because in Him is
perfect peace.

Day Four

THE PATHWAY TO PEACE

Have you ever obsessed over something you were worried about to the point that you couldn't fall asleep and woke up tired the next day? Then you realized it wasn't a big deal at all? I've been there too. Looking back, I can't believe how over-focused I became on something that wasn't that important in the grand scheme of life.

Whether our fears are overblown or completely appropriate because life has thrown us some curveballs, most of us struggle to find peace in our problems. Isaiah's message gives us hope that we can make internal choices that lead to peace when we face external forces that tempt us to worry.

EXTERNAL FORCES

> **READ ISAIAH 7:1-2.** Describe how the king of Judah and his people responded to the external forces coming against them.

King Ahaz faced threats from two countries. One of these was Judah's own family. Israel was the Northern Kingdom made of ten tribes that separated from Judah after Solomon's reign. Sometimes when our pain comes from unexpected places—like family, friends, or a church or school we thought was safe—our fears can feel magnified.

> What would you identify as a current challenge coming from external forces? What stressors are threatening your peace right now?

We all have challenges from external forces, whether they're happening directly to us or impacting us through the people we love. Maybe your situation revolves around a family situation, a broken friendship or gossip, or even not making a specific team or getting into a certain school and has left you feeling like the people of Judah—"shaking in a storm" (v. 2). So, what do we do when we feel the impact of outside forces tossing us about in life?

> **READ ISAIAH 7:3-9.** What did Isaiah tell the king to stop doing in verse 4?

> According to verse 9, what needed to happen for the Lord to make him stand firm?

The Lord told Ahaz to stop worrying. "Do not fear" is a command issued often throughout Scripture. Philippians 4:6 tells us "don't worry about anything." That sounds so good, but how do we do that? Like when we can't sleep, can't stop recycling our thoughts and emotions, and feel like peace is a luxury we aren't afforded in our families, our friendships, our school, and so on? One commentator summarized God's instruction to stand firm in faith as "trust or bust!"[12]

> As you reflect on the challenge you identified earlier, what are the alternatives to trusting God?

When I choose not to trust, I often revert to worry, excessive planning, or complaining about the problem to others. I could definitely put all those in the "bust" category!

But the Lord doesn't leave us without help in these moments. He wants to help us stand firm in our faith as He instructed Ahaz to do when facing his fears.

READ ISAIAH 8. Record in the chart below what you learn about God's offer to care for His people and His instructions to help them grow in trust. (I did the first ones for you. Answers will vary by translation.)

GOD'S CARE FOR HIS PEOPLE	GOD'S INSTRUCTIONS
Verse 6: Provided gently flowing waters	Verse 11: Don't think like everyone else (NLT). Don't follow the way of this people (NIV). Don't walk in the way of this people (ESV).
Verse 10:	Verse 12:
Verse 14:	Verse 13:
	Verse 16:
	Verse 17:
	Verse 19:
	Verse 20:

God longed to care for His people like gently flowing waters. He was with them and was a place of safety for them. He alone could be their pathway to peace, yet so many times they rejected Him. They didn't trust Him to care for them and instead looked to human strength, false gods, and mediums for guidance.

INTERNAL CHOICES

READ ISAIAH 26:3. What are some practical ways to fix your thoughts on the Lord when you find yourself shaken by external forces?

Here are a few ideas I've implemented when I find myself struggling to embrace God's peace in the midst of a storm: Write a list of God's attributes or names in my journal. Go for a walk or change my physical posture to redirect my body and mind. Call or text a friend and ask her to pray for my mental focus to shift.

We may not have a prophet who can tell us exactly what the future holds, but we can think differently than others with reasoned responses rather than knee-jerk reactions.

We can decide to stop striving and trust God. When we do, we'll find the power to obey commands like "stop worrying," "don't fear," and "have faith," even when life is scary. We can find perfect peace when we fix our thoughts on Him. I hope that no matter what type of challenge you are facing today, you can find peace in knowing God loves you and longs to be your Defender!

DAILY WRAP-UP

Today we focused on this truth: *We can trust God because in Him is perfect peace.* How would you summarize your personal takeaway from today's study?

MEMORY VERSE ACTIVITY

Attempt to write out Isaiah 1:18 from memory, then check to see how you did.

BIG IDEA
We can trust
God because
He is with us.

Day Five

IMMANUEL, GOD WITH US

After spending large amounts of time with people—even people I dearly love—I need a break. I want to shut myself in my room with a "keep out" sign on the door. But I've also experienced the flip side—loneliness—when my family is out of the house or busy. I guess too much of a good thing is true even for introverts! Following God doesn't immunize us against feelings of loneliness, either. They can even creep into our relationship with the Lord.

When God seems a million miles away or when our prayers feel like they are hitting the ceiling, we can encounter spiritual loneliness. During these seasons, we might entertain questions like:

- *Is the Lord still with me?*
- *How can I trust that He is still here even when I've messed up again, disappointed people I love, or questioned my beliefs?*
- *What should I do in moments when I can't sense God's nearness?*

If someone came to you with these types of questions, how would you advise them?

As we read Isaiah's words today, we will draw out facts that will help us trust God when our feelings aren't on board. Even when we don't sense God at work, He is. He is Immanuel, God with us. We just need to rediscover what we already have: a God who went to great lengths to redeem His relationship with His people.

A SIGN OF HOPE

READ ISAIAH 7:10-25. Draw a line from the person to the action.

Lord (vv. 10-11) Will conceive a child and call Him Immanuel

Ahaz (v. 12) Will feel fortunate to have a cow and two sheep or goats left

Isaiah (v. 13) Sent a message through the prophet Isaiah to Ahaz to ask for a sign

Virgin (v. 14) Refused to ask for a sign as the Lord instructed

Farmer (v. 21) Asked Ahaz why he was exhausting the Lord's patience

The apostle Paul described people like Ahaz when he wrote, "They will act religious, but they will reject the power that could make them godly. Stay away from people like that!" (2 Tim. 3:5).

Testing God was forbidden in the law (Deut. 6:16), but Ahaz twisted the command rather than accepting God's invitation in faith. This exasperated Isaiah. It isn't testing God to do as He says! Although Ahaz didn't specify a sign, the Lord gave him one anyway.

I always thought this prophecy regarding a virgin was about Jesus the Messiah, and it definitely was fulfilled in Christ. However, it was also fulfilled for the original readers of Isaiah's message: only a year or two after the prophecy was given the nations of Syria and Israel (the ones who threatened Judah) were destroyed by Assyria (Isa. 7:16). Although we don't know the identity of the mother or child, the time frame of Isaiah's sign fit with historical events. We also know this sign had future implications. One commentator described his opinion this way, "I believe that the sign as originally given had a single meaning but a double significance. Its meaning is that God is with us and we need not fear what other human beings may do to us."[13]

The verse was significant to Ahaz as a challenge not to seek alliances with foreign nations like Assyria for help since God was with him. But the Gospel of Matthew also helps us see its fulfillment in the birth of Jesus.

READ MATTHEW 1:21-23. How does the angel's message to Joseph give insight into Isaiah's words?

Signs like the one given in Isaiah 7:14 confirm God's long-term plan and commitment to His people. One scholar described the fullness of meaning in Matthew's words as "inspired reapplications of the inspired words."[14] The meaning is clear for Isaiah's day, Matthew's day, and ours: God is with us.

Consider what the Messiah's name—Immanuel—means for you. How does it affect you to know God is with you today in whatever circumstances you're facing?

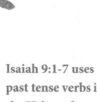

Isaiah 9:1-7 uses past tense verbs in the Hebrew because Isaiah's hope was so certain, he wrote as though it had already happened.[15]

LIGHT FOR OUR DARKNESS

READ ISAIAH 9:1-7.

What would the people see (vv. 1-2)?

What would be broken (v. 4)?

What names were given for the child (v. 6)?

What would His government be like? What would make this happen (v. 7)?

Let's look closer at the names for the Promised One found in verse 6 and what they reveal to us about His character:

- **Wonderful Counselor** literally means "wonder-planner" or "wonder-working planner."[16]
- **Mighty God** emphasizes power like that of a champion in battle.

- **Everlasting Father** may seem an odd title for the Son of God, but it highlights the Messiah's timeless concern, care, and discipline of His people.[17]
- **Prince of Peace** suggests an army commander, but unlike most princes, this commander's ultimate goal is peace.

Put a star next to the name you needed to hear today. Why did you choose that name?

How did the passages we read today land in your soul? Record any thoughts, questions, or insights you gained from Isaiah 9:1-7.

I don't know what you're walking through right now, but I'm sure there have been times when you could relate to living in a land that feels dark (Isa. 9:2). The darkness isn't only "out there" in the world. We often personally trudge through grief, complicated relationships, or other trials that can leave us in a dark place. When we focus our eyes on Jesus, we make our fundamental reality one that's focused on hope.

At the heart of Isaiah's message is the hope of the gospel: God sent His only Son, Jesus, to earth, and He offered the perfect sacrifice—Jesus's very life—to cleanse us from our sins: And because Jesus went into death with us, He can bring us out with Him.[18]

MEMORY VERSE
Write down or say aloud Isaiah 1:18 from memory.

DAILY WRAP-UP

Today we focused on this truth: *We can trust God because He is with us.* How would you summarize your personal takeaway from today's study?

Session Two
GROUP TIME

REVIEW
Use the following Scripture passages and questions to discuss what you learned in your personal Bible study.

Recall the Big Idea for each of the five days of study.

Read Isaiah 1:10-15. Talk about how we might see hypocrisy today.

Read Isaiah 1:16-17. Name the changes God asks His people to make to restore their relationship with Him. What might it look like for a person to do these things today?

Review the Names of God chart on page 22. Tell which names you highlighted and why.

Describe the challenges you mentioned on Day Four. Talk about the ways someone might be tempted to address this without trusting God. How does trusting God change everything?

Review the chart on page 28. Share what way God cares for His people that stood out most to you.

Share with the group your favorite personal takeaway from all five days of personal study and how it helps you trust God.

MEMORIZE
Assign each girl a word or phrase of Isaiah 1:18. Popcorn read the verse one word or phrase at a time. Go through it several times this way, then recite the full verse together.

WATCH

Use the fill-in-the-blanks and note-taking space as you watch the Session 2 teaching video together as a group.

We have to let God be _____ so that we can be _____ to Him.

We want to look at God's faithfulness in the _____ to help us trust Him in the _____.

God's invitation to us is to fill the gap with _____.

We can trust God and trust His character because He is _____ and _____.

Isaiah didn't say, "_____ is me." He said, "_____ is me."

Our God is _____ but He is in complete _____.

God says religious _____ won't fix the spiritual rot in your soul. He's after our _____.

WOW: _____

WOE: _____

NOTES

PRAY

God, You are sovereign and I know I can trust You. Help me surrender my heart, my life, and my plans fully to You.

TRUST *God's* CALENDAR

SESSION THREE

Trusting God's timing sounds good on paper, but it isn't so easy when God's calendar and ours don't seem to line up. Our culture has done everything possible to eliminate waiting.

We can stream a movie, order take-out food, or buy something with a few simple clicks and get it that same day! Waiting on God can be challenging when it may seem like He doesn't respond as fast as Amazon®.

Yet Isaiah reminds us that God is never early, and He is never late. He is always right on time. When we get impatient and strive more, we often find ourselves trusting less. This week we'll learn from King Hezekiah some lessons about trusting God's calendar in our own lives. Sometimes Hezekiah got it right, and other times he took a short-sighted view. As we explore Isaiah's message together, we'll learn to surrender our timelines to trust that our Creator knows the best timing for our moves, events, education, reconciliations, health, and every other agenda we are pushing in our lives and the lives of those we love.

So the Lord must wait for you to come to him so he can show you his love and compassion. For the Lord is a faithful God. Blessed are those who wait for his help.

ISAIAH 30:18

BIG IDEA

In the waiting period between our trouble and God's rescue, we pray.

Day One

WAITING AND PRAYING

Have you ever gone through a long period of waiting that challenged your trust in the Lord? Explain.

This week our focus in Isaiah will center around trusting God's calendar, which means surrendering to His timing over ours. When God doesn't act as quickly as we'd like, we can revert to striving in our human strength to get what we want rather than seeking to trust Him. For me that often looks like freaking out (worry, fear) or excessive planning.

What would you add to this list of reactions you have when God doesn't seem to be working on your timetable?

King Hezekiah's story shows us one example of what it looks like to trust God's plan even when we face circumstances that threaten our security. Let's briefly review the biblical timeline that leads up to Hezekiah:

930 BC	729/8 BC	722 BC	715 BC	701 BC
The twelve tribes of Israel split into the Northern Kingdom of Israel and the Southern Kingdom of Judah.[1]	King Ahaz's son Hezekiah began to reign in Judah (likely alongside his father as co-regent).[2]	Assyria conquered and exiled the Northern Kingdom of Israel (2 Kings 18:11-12).[3]	King Ahaz died and Hezekiah reigned solo in Judah.[4]	Hezekiah gave the Assyrians all of Judah's silver and gold to keep them from invading but they still sent an army to threaten attack if they would not agree to exile (2 Kings 18:14-16).[5]

In spite of Hezekiah's payoff, the commander of the Assyrian army came to threaten Judah during the days of Isaiah. This is the historical backdrop as we enter the scene of Isaiah 36.

READ ISAIAH 36:1-22. Then circle in your Bible or highlight in the list below the threats Judah faced that seem scariest to you.

The Assyrian army sent by Sennacherib was "huge" (v. 2). The commander spoke threatening words to cause fear and undermine trust in Yahweh—the God of Israel. He referenced trusting in the Lord seven times (vv. 4-7, 9, 15) and used these arguments:

- Words won't help you against military might (vv. 4-6);
- God is mad at you for getting rid of His altars (v. 7);
- God called our nation to punish you (v. 10);
- Your leaders can't be trusted because Hezekiah is deceiving you to trust in a God who can't rescue (vv. 14-16);
- Slavery is the best option for you (vv. 16-17);
- Look around you at the other nations we've defeated for evidence that there is no way out (vv. 18-19).

These tactics remind us of those used by another enemy of the Lord. Like the field commander, Satan often uses one argument after another hoping to leave his victims feeling hopeless and helpless. You've probably never faced armies shouting threats, but maybe your inner dialogue has included some version of these same lies.

Read the following statements and put a star next to any that sound familiar, or add another statement related to your own personal battles to trust the Lord.

- Make a backup plan in case God doesn't come through.
- God is mad at you for messing up, so you can't count on Him.
- Your spiritual leaders can't be trusted. They probably have their own agendas.
- Slavery to sin is normal; you'll never overcome these temptations.
- No one else has won these battles so neither will you.
-

Lies of the enemy show themselves in a variety of ways and waiting on the Lord doesn't always seem like the best option. So, what should we do during the time between the threat of trouble and God's rescue?

READ ISAIAH 37:1-4. Identify the responses Hezekiah displayed. Which response might you be able to incorporate in your life?

Hezekiah didn't put on a happy face and pretend everything was fine. His faith in God led him to mourn, ask for prayer, and seek God's word through the prophet Isaiah. Hezekiah's example reminds us that trusting God doesn't mean we won't experience grief.

"Except for David and Solomon, no king of Judah is given more attention or commendation in Scripture than Hezekiah."[6]

READ ISAIAH 37:5-7. Summarize Isaiah's message from the Lord.

Hezekiah had a choice. He could trust the word of God spoken by Isaiah or try to fix the problem on his own. This is often the tension for me. I want to believe God's promises, but I struggle in the place between the promise and the rescue—especially if that season drags on.

READ ISAIAH 37:15-20. Record in the chart below Hezekiah's praises and requests.

PRAISE (NAMES, CHARACTER, POWER, ETC.)	REQUESTS
Verse 16	Verse 17
Verse 20	Verse 20

God answered Hezekiah's prayer. Isaiah prophesied against Assyria for the remainder of the chapter. We can trust God in our seasons of waiting, knowing that He is working even when we don't feel it. Spend some time considering anywhere your trust feels threatened. You may not feel like you are facing anything in your life right now like Hezekiah battled. Yet when you learn to trust God with the small things, you will be prepared to trust Him during your own times of crisis.

Write a two-part prayer, first praising God and then making specific requests.

Praise:

Requests:

Hezekiah stayed the course, trusting God even when the situation seemed impossible. He knew other kingdoms failed against Assyria because their gods weren't real. God sent an angel into "the Assyrian camp and killed 185,000 Assyrian soldiers" (Isa. 37:36). This great loss caused King Sennacherib to return home where his sons killed him with swords while he was worshiping in the temple of his false god Nisroch (v. 38).

God intervened according to His plan, and yet at the same time responded to Hezekiah's prayer. I wonder if Hezekiah would look back on his season of trouble and acknowledge an intimacy with God that desperation can produce. While waiting seasons aren't usually my favorite, they are a place where trust can grow.

DAILY WRAP-UP

Today we focused on this truth: *In the waiting period between our trouble and God's rescue, we pray.* **How would you summarize your personal takeaway from today's study?**

PRAYER

Lord, help me wait patiently and expectantly. When troubles threaten my trust in You, remind me to pray, seek Your Word, and enlist spiritual support instead of freaking out and planning excessively. I know Your calendar is better than mine. Help me live that truth when the tyranny of the urgent overwhelms me. In Jesus's name, amen.

MEMORY VERSE

Read Isaiah 30:18 aloud three times. You can find it printed on page 37.

BIG IDEA
Prayer can change
even the most
established timelines.

Day Two
CHANGING TIMELINES

My prayer habits have always been a struggle. The gap between my desire and actual execution when it comes to prayer confuses me. The open-ended amount of time prayer may take causes me to put it off for later, and too many times later never comes. I recently made some prayer progress by setting alarms on my phone for shorter blocks of prayer throughout the day. Somehow having an end time helps me get started. This might not be a problem for you, but having a system helped my prayer goals become more in line with reality.

Describe your prayer practices, including your ideal and your reality:

• What you want your prayer life to look like:

• Your current prayer routines:

To trust God more, we need a fresh vision that prayer changes things— even events on our calendars. Have you ever been confused about Bible verses that say God never changes His mind and then read stories in the Bible where it seemed like He did? Or wondered about the connection between faith and action as you try to walk in God's ways? We'll consider these questions and more as we look at Hezekiah's example today.

PRAYER FULFILLS GOD'S PLAN

READ ISAIAH 38:1-8. Briefly describe Hezekiah's sickness and recovery in your own words.

Hezekiah was literally up against a wall. In that moment he probably experienced confusion as well as grief. Hezekiah was from David's line, and he knew God's promise of a descendant of David reigning on the throne of Judah forever (2 Sam. 7:16). Yet he did not have a son at that point in his life.[7] As the leader of a nation, he would've understood how no clear succession plan and threats of Assyrian invasion could cause instability in the kingdom.[8]

When Hezekiah prayed, the Lord responded. This is God's unchanging character and plan. When people humble themselves and pray, He acts!

Focus on Isaiah 38:5-6. Underline the verbs God used.

God promised He would act on behalf of Hezekiah and His people. Just as the Lord heard Hezekiah's prayers, He also hears ours. God invites us to come boldly before His throne and assures us we will find mercy there (Heb. 4:16). Isaiah 38 and many other examples in Scripture reveal God responding with action to the prayers of His people. We pray because God fulfills His plan of responding to those who seek Him.

While we marvel at this story, it does bring up complicated questions like, *Can prayer change God's mind? If God has a predetermined plan, why pray at all? Why does God answer some prayers and not others?* Although we could spend pages and pages trying to unpack exactly how God's sovereignty and our prayer work together, for now we will leave it at this: We pray because we know God's unchanging character, and because He invites us to ask boldly in faith for anything (Mark 11:24). Throughout Scripture we see that the Lord responds to humble prayers of righteous people (Ex. 32:9-14; 2 Chron. 7:14; Jas. 5:16). The key is to trust Him with the outcome.

The account of Hezekiah's sickness and recovery in Isaiah 38:7-8 also appears in 2 Kings 20. We glean an additional detail that Hezekiah was given a choice whether the shadow would move backward or forward in God's sign of the sundial (2 Kings 20:9-11).

"The sundial was probably a pillar whose shadow marked the hours on a double set of stairs."[9]

One commentator said it this way: God "invites us to tell him what we think our needs are because our trust is deepened as we see God providing the very things we asked for. But that does not mean that we demand he work for us. It means we lay our supposed needs at his feet for him to supply as he sees best. This kind of prayer is no longer an exercise in manipulation. Now it is a conversation between a trusting child and a loving Father."[10]

If a friend asked, how would you answer the following question: "If God's will is already established, then why should we pray?"

FAITH AND ACTION OFTEN COME TOGETHER IN PRAYER

READ ISAIAH 38:21-22. What did Isaiah tell the servants to spread over Hezekiah's boil to help him recover (v. 21)? What did Hezekiah ask to prove he would be made well (v. 22)?

What do you learn about prayer from these verses?

Praying in faith doesn't mean we don't participate in the answer. Sometimes I have thought taking action alongside prayer indicated that I didn't trust God to answer. In Hezekiah's story, action went hand in hand with prayer. We can pray for healing and take medicine. We can pray to pass a test and study hard. It doesn't have to be one or the other.

Another principle I found in these verses was Hezekiah's desire for a sign. He had faith but also needed reassurance. He models for us the coupling of our human weakness with the power of trusting the Lord. We can believe but ask God to help our unbelief (Mark 9:24). Now let's read Hezekiah's prayer in response to healing in his life.

POWERFUL PRAYERS INCLUDE REFLECTION

READ ISAIAH 38:9-20. Write down one or two lines of Hezekiah's prayer poem that stand out to you.

I appreciate how Hezekiah acknowledged the desperation we can experience in prayer in verse 14. Hezekiah reflected on his emotions with authenticity. He didn't try to minimize what he felt.

When have you cried out to God like this?

While the Hebrew word used in Isaiah 38:9 for Hezekiah's prayer is *miktab,* which means "writing," many commentators refer to it as a psalm or poem because it parallels the poetic style of a Hebrew lament.[11] The NLT used the word "poem" for *miktab,* likely because of its construction.

Prayer doesn't have to be poetry, and I'll admit my journal entries look more like stream of consciousness than anything poetic. What Hezekiah's prayer poem reveals to us is that prayer should include reflection, regardless of how poetic it sounds. He took time to consider, practice gratitude, and learn from his experience. He reflected on his thoughts and emotions. Hezekiah helps us know that we don't need desperation to pray. On the other side of trials, we can reflect and praise.

When have you praised God after He brought you through a tough situation?

If we really believe prayer changes things, then we won't be so quick to skip it. We may not understand everything about how prayer works, but I hope Hezekiah's experience inspires us toward a more intense and consistent prayer life.

Let's take a few moments to do that now. Reflect on your relationship with the Lord. Use the acrostic PRAY to write four lines to the Lord, starting each sentence with a word beginning with these letters:

P

R

A

Y

DAILY WRAP-UP

Today we focused on this truth: *Prayer can change even the most established timelines.* How would you summarize your personal takeaway from today's study?

Day Three

A LONG-TERM MINDSET

Can you think of a season when you experienced God's nearness in your life? Write down anything that comes to mind.

SCRIPTURE FOCUS
Isaiah 39

BIG IDEA
Trust is intended to be a way of life, not an antidote for crisis.

So far, we've been inspired by Hezekiah's trust in the Lord and poetic prayers. In Isaiah 39, we will uncover his mistake in failing to maintain a long-term mindset. After a supernatural healing, he wasn't careful in considering how his decisions would impact the future. We will be reminded again today that a long-term mindset impacts short-term decisions. Isaiah teaches us that trust in God should be a lifelong expression rather than a means of getting out of crisis.

Today's chapter hints toward events that will occur more than one hundred years into Judah's future of Babylonian exile, which occurred in 586 BC.[12]

AVOID DISTRACTIONS

READ ISAIAH 39:1-8. What country did Merodach-baladan reign over as king? Why did he send an envoy and a gift to Hezekiah (v. 1)?

How did Hezekiah respond to the envoy's arrival (v. 2)?

What questions did Isaiah ask Hezekiah, and how did Hezekiah respond (vv. 3-4)?

What did Isaiah prophesy would happen, and what was Hezekiah's response to the prophecy (vv. 5-8)?

The letters sent by the king of Babylon likely contained a hidden agenda. He wanted Hezekiah to join him in the fight against Assyria. The Lord had already assured Hezekiah of rescue from Assyria (Isa. 38:6). Hezekiah could have responded to the letters and the envoy politely, sharing with them the power of God and His promise to save them.

Instead, Hezekiah seemed to be thrilled by the attention. While we can't assume Hezekiah's exact thoughts, we do know he became self-absorbed after the Lord healed him instead of trusting the Lord (Isa. 39:2).

AVOID SHORT-SIGHTEDNESS

READ 2 CHRONICLES 32:24-31. List two or three additional insights we find from this passage.

"The LORD Almighty," the title for God used by Isaiah in verse 5 of the NIV, "lays emphasis on the infinite resources used by the Lord in his acts of power. Hezekiah's own resources may have seemed great to him, but those of the Lord were far greater."[13]

In your opinion, what was wrong with Hezekiah's mindset at this time in his life?

You might say Hezekiah didn't focus on the Lord and the future impact of his decisions. He was living in the moment possibly with pride, overconfidence, and forgetfulness of God's sovereign plan. The Lord healed him and promised to protect the nation, but when the crisis ended, Hezekiah seemed to get caught up in his possessions. Isaiah's questions were meant to help him see his trust in man rather than God for protection. Yet Hezekiah responded by being defensive instead of humble.

REREAD ISAIAH 39:5-8. How did Hezekiah's response reveal his short-sightedness?

We get a glimpse into Hezekiah's mindset in Isaiah 39:8b, "For the king was thinking, 'At least there will be peace and security during my lifetime.'" Again, he was thinking only of his personal pain for the moment. Avoiding pain is our human nature, but Hezekiah's concern for himself reveals his lack of foresight. He didn't grieve for his offspring or seem too concerned about his legacy but instead rested in his own comfort.

ADOPT A LONG-TERM MINDSET

We want to develop a long-term mindset that impacts our short-term decisions so we can avoid falling into the overconfidence of Hezekiah. We don't only want to trust the Lord when things in our lives are awful. Instead, we want to make trusting the Lord a way of life that guides us in good times and on difficult days. Let's practice this together.

Make a short list of decisions you will make today and in the future. (These can be as simple as what you will eat or what you post on social media or more significant things like choosing a college. Try to include a mix of small and big decisions in your responses.)

TODAY	THIS WEEK	IN THE COMING MONTHS

PRAYER

Lord, I don't want to get stuck in the moment. Help me seek You whether I have a desperate need, a great blessing, or the in-between mundane. I know my tendency to drift away from trusting You and striving in my own strength. As I make decisions today, tomorrow, and into the future, help me consider You in each one. In Jesus's name, amen.

MEMORY VERSE

Write down Isaiah 30:18. Also record one thought you have as you read over this verse.

Now look back over what you've written and put a star by the one that weighs most heavily on you—whether it's a daily choice or a one-time decision. Consider the impact of your choice in one month, one year, ten years, and even into eternity. How might taking a long-term mindset influence the choice you marked?

If you get stuck, here are some examples: *How might the decision to pray regularly or not pray regularly impact your spiritual growth? How might your daily study habits affect your grades? How might having more or less screen-time affect your health and relationships?"*

Taking a long-term mindset is recognized even in secular circles. Brian Tracy wrote in his book *Eat That Frog*, "Your attitude toward time, your 'time horizon,' has an enormous impact on your behavior and your choices. People who take a long-term view of their lives and careers seem to make much better decisions about their time and activities than people who give very little thought to the future."[14] If only Hezekiah could have maintained a "time horizon" with eternity in mind, he likely would have thanked the Babylonians for their well-wishes and turned again to the Lord to sustain him.

Having a long-term mindset impacts our lives here on earth and reflects the heart of the gospel message. Believing Jesus came to reconcile us to the Father because of our sin stretches us to think not just about today but about what will matter in eternity.

DAILY WRAP-UP

Today we focused on this truth: *Trust is intended to be a way of life, not an antidote for crisis.* How would you summarize your personal takeaway from today's study?

Day Four

THE POWER OF REFLECTION

How do you keep track of what's going on in your life? Do your parents keep a calendar and tell you where to show up when? Or are you keeping up with it on your own, using a calendar, planner, or app?

No matter how you manage your time, most of us would admit we struggle to trust God's calendar. The Lord calls us to plan wisely (Ps. 90:12). We all must make decisions about our routines and time commitments, including school activities, sports, rest, relationships, hobbies, social media, and so on. But we all know that our best laid plans often get hijacked by emergencies, unexpected circumstances, or even global pandemics!

As we try to trust God's calendar, we need wisdom to discern what to add to ours. Isaiah's message gives us practical insights that will help us make plans while holding them loosely as we anticipate divine interventions.

REMEMBER WHAT GOD HAS DONE IN THE PAST

READ ISAIAH 46. How long did God say He has cared for His people? How long did God say He would care for them (vv. 3-4)?

What command did God issue regarding the past (vv. 8-9)?

What did the Lord remind them about the future (v. 10)?

BIG IDEA
Remember what the Lord has done in the past so you can trust Him in the present.

Proverbs 16:9 reminds us, "We can make our plans, but the LORD determines our steps."

"All references so far made in the prophecy of Isaiah to pagan deities or idols have been general. Here, Isaiah named the two great gods of Babylon: Bel (also called Marduk) and Nebo."[15]

Notice how the gods of Babylon had to be carried (v. 1), but the Lord said He would carry His people (v. 4). Isaiah used this play on words to remind his readers that idols were man-made objects. They weren't real. Without making an effort to remember, we can also get swept into the superficial thinking of our culture. What we believe drives how we prioritize our time.

The Lord challenged His people to remember what He had done in the past so they would trust Him instead of worthless idols. These reminders weren't intended only for the original audience. The Lord also calls us to remember His work in our own stories.

> Name ways the Lord has cared for you in the past.
> These don't have to be major moments. Try to think
> of times God provided, comforted, spoke, or affirmed
> even in small ways.

•

•

•

"Most commentators consider chapter 47 to be a self-contained poem."[16]

REFLECT ON CHOICES IN THE PRESENT

When we remember what the Lord has done in our lives in the past, it can help us trust Him today. God not only foretold of Babylon's victory over Judah but also their ultimate fall.

> READ ISAIAH 47:1-10. Make notes of the Lord's
> charges against Babylon.

Babylon showed Judah "no mercy" (v. 6). They loved pleasure and felt secure in their wickedness (vv. 8,10). They relied on their own wisdom and knowledge, which led them astray (v. 10). We will hit some of these themes later in our study of Isaiah, but for our purposes today, we will focus on verse 7b.

READ ISAIAH 47:7b in the following four translations. Circle all the words that begin with the letter R.

You did not reflect on your actions
or think about their consequences (NLT).

But you did not consider these things
or reflect on what might happen (NIV).

So that you did not lay these things
to heart or remember their end (ESV).

These things you did not consider
Nor remember the outcome of them (NASB).

We want to remember what God has done in the past, but we also need to reflect on our choices in the present. The Lord punished Babylon for acting thoughtlessly. He calls us to pause in our busy days to think about what we are doing, why we are doing it, and how it will impact others.

Glance over your schedule for the next seven days and take some time to reflect on these questions:

How are you planning to spend your time in the coming week?

What interruptions might you anticipate?

Is there anything you sense the Lord would add or eliminate from your plan?

After you reflect, jot down any insights, ideas, or questions.

I've found that taking just five or ten minutes to stop, pray, and remember what I'm doing and why I'm doing it has been so helpful. You may reflect differently, but all of us can listen to the Lord's call to think more deeply.

When Jesus was accused of breaking the Sabbath (by healing of all things), He challenged people not to get caught in the shallow end of God's plan. He said, "Look beneath the surface so you can judge correctly" (John 7:24). This command summarizes God's message through Isaiah about reflecting on our actions. God wants us to be mindful of living for Him instead of just going through the motions of Christianity.

REAFFIRM GOD'S GOODNESS FOR THE FUTURE

The Lord not only calls us to remember the past and reflect on the present but also to look toward the future. A future with God is a future with hope. God entrusted Isaiah with details of the Babylonian exile, punishment, and return. Isaiah also gave the people glimpses of God's future goodness to them. Whether we are in a season of prosperity or desperation, we can all look to the future with excitement.

READ ISAIAH 51:9-16. Fill in the blanks with a one-word answer to complete each sentence regarding the future for God's people as recorded in verse 11. (I've used the NLT Bible version.)

"Those who have been ransomed [rescued, redeemed] by the LORD will _____. They will enter Jerusalem [Zion] _____, crowned with everlasting _____. Sorrow and mourning will _____, and they will be filled with joy and gladness."

Before the future captivity would unfold, the Lord wanted the people to know He would rescue them. He gave them a peek at His divine calendar so they could be prepared and trust Him through the process.

But like many of us, the Israelites quickly forgot. Note how God reminded them of ...

- what He had done in the past (v. 13)

- His present power (v. 15)

- what they could expect in the future (v. 15)

You may or may not be of Jewish descent, but if you have turned from your sin and turned to God, then you belong to Him. Isaiah's words teach us the importance of trusting God's calendar. We remember the past, reflect in the present, and reaffirm the future hope in God's good plans for our lives.

When you attach your trust to God's eternal blessings rather than ease, convenience, and trouble-free circumstances here on earth, you can more easily surrender your calendar to His control. God longs to walk with you through each and every day, whether it is marked with difficulty or celebration.

Today's passages helped me process through the tension I feel between these two statements:

- God calls me to plan wisely.
- God calls me to trust His plan.

I believe we reconcile both of these truths as we loosen our grip on our own agendas. I'm asking the Lord to show me how to implement reflection in my life, and I hope He is stirring your heart as well.

DAILY WRAP-UP

Today we focused on this truth: *Remember what the Lord has done in the past so you can trust Him in the present.* **How would you summarize your personal takeaway from today's study?**

BIG IDEA
We can trust God's
timing because He
sent His Son, Jesus,
just as He promised.

Day Five

WRITTEN ON HIS PALM

**When have you forgotten to show up for something
or shown up late?**

In our study today, we'll find that thankfully the Lord doesn't have this
same struggle. He has never forgotten anything, ever—except that He
chooses to forget about our sin (Isa. 43:25). It may feel like He doesn't
always respond to our prayers or intervene when we think He should,
but He certainly has not forgotten about us.

I hope reading Isaiah 49 will remind you of the Lord's faithfulness and
help you trust His timing when it comes to the details of your life. If He
knew just the right moment to send His Son into the world, you can trust
Him with your calendar as well.

THE SERVANT MESSIAH

Isaiah contains four
Servant Songs found
in Isaiah 42:1-4;
49:1-6; 50:4-11; and
52:13–53:12. Each
one makes reference
to the Servant of the
Lord, whom we know
as Jesus, the promised
Messiah. These
passages highlight
the Messiah's role as
a Suffering Servant
rather than a
conquering King.

Before we dig into the passage, let's look at some background
information. In the chapters leading up to chapter 49, Isaiah prophesied
regarding Israel's exile to Babylon and the fall of Babylon to King Cyrus
of Persia. Isaiah called Cyrus by name 170 years before he invaded
Babylon (Isa. 44:28).[17] Some have used this prophetic detail to question
the date and authorship of Isaiah by wondering how the prophet could
have known these specifics about Cyrus and the rise of the Persian
Empire. However, these references provide no problem for those
of us who believe Isaiah's writings to be a divine work inspired by a
supernatural God who sits outside of time and knows all things.

In chapter 49, the language shifts from describing a human king to giving
Messianic references. Isaiah spoke of One who would come to rescue not
just God's people but the entire world!

READ ISAIAH 49:1-7. Circle the multiple-choice letter that best answers each question.

1. Whom does the Lord's servant address in verse 1?
    A. Those who live in Judah
    B. The Babylonians
    C. All those living far away (islands, coastlands)

2. What was the servant's commission in verses 5-6?
    A. To bring Israel back to the Lord
    B. To be a light to the Gentiles and bring salvation to the ends of the earth
    C. Both A and B

3. How is the servant described in regard to the nations in verse 7?
    A. Royal and noble
    B. Forgetful and lazy
    C. Trendy and cool

List some words that describe how the servant in these verses reminds you of Jesus.

"The Jewish nation was called to glorify God and be a light to the Gentiles, but they failed in their mission. This is why Messiah is called 'Israel' in Isaiah 49:3: He did the work that Israel was supposed to do."[18]

READ THE FOLLOWING COMPLEMENTARY PASSAGES in your Bible and circle any words or phrases that remind you of Isaiah 49:1-7.

1. Luke 2:32 (Simeon's prophecy at Christ's birth)
2. Acts 13:47 (Paul preaching the gospel to Gentiles)
3. Isaiah 53:3 (Isaiah writing a messianic prophecy)

Through Isaiah, the Redeemer of Israel told His people about their future rescue from exile in Babylon, but He also hinted at a much greater fulfillment when Jesus would come to earth in human form to die for our sins. The original audience wouldn't live long enough to see the exile or rescue of God's people—or the birth of Christ. Yet God revealed glimpses so they could see His design and live with hope and trust in Him.

THE SHEPHERD MESSIAH

READ ISAIAH 49:8-26. When did the Lord say He would respond (v. 8)?

What would He say to the prisoners? What would He say to those in darkness (v. 9)?

What did Jerusalem (or Zion) say, and how did the Lord respond (vv. 14-15)?

What has the Lord written on the palms of His hands (v. 16)?

What will the people and the nations know after all this happens (vv. 23,26)?

Highlight the illustrations that stood out to you from these promises.

In this poetic Servant Song, we find the Lord using illustrations of a shepherd leading his people beside cool water, a nursing mother never forgetting her child, a courageous warrior, and a God who has written our names in the palm of His hand. Jesus is the Shepherd who leaves the ninety-nine to go after the one lost sheep (Matt. 18:12-14). The Lord said, "I will fight those who fight you, and I will save your children" (Isa. 49:25b).

All of these pictures remind us of God's incredible love for His people, but the one image that really tugs at my emotions is God's engraving of our names in the palm of His hand. Pastor Warren Wiersbe said, "The word *engraved* means 'to cut into' signifying its permanence."[19] This writing wasn't something like a pencil, pen, or even a Sharpie® marker; it was a permanent signature, often chiseled in stone. Take a minute to let that sink in. These verses were not just for the nation of Israel. Yahweh is not the God of the Jews but the God of the entire world. This means He knows your name, your questions, and what you're waiting for.

As you consider these truths, write your name in the palm below.

God is faithful to do what He says He will do at just the right time. He sent His Servant, Jesus, to save us from our sin. His hand is extended toward us.

REREAD ISAIAH 30:18 in your Bible and underline what God is waiting to show you.

The Lord isn't waiting to punish us; He's waiting to show us His love and compassion. He's waiting for us to come to Him, and He says we are blessed when we wait for His help.

READ 2 CORINTHIANS 6:2 in your Bible.

As Paul said in 2 Corinthians 6:2, if you've never confessed with your mouth and believed in your heart that Jesus is the Messiah, today is the day! If you've embraced this truth already, maybe today is a fresh reminder of God's perfect timing. Even when we can't see or feel it, God works out His perfect plan in His perfect timing.

DAILY WRAP-UP

Today we focused on this truth: *We can trust God's timing because He sent His Son, Jesus, just as He promised.* How would you summarize your personal takeaway from today's study?

PRAYER

God, thank You for sending Your Son, the despised and rejected Servant who brought light into my life! It blows my mind to think that my name is written in the palm of Your hand. Give me patience to be a better waiter. Help me trust that Your faithful timing is best. In Jesus's name, amen.

MEMORY VERSE
Write down or say aloud Isaiah 30:18 from memory.

Session Three
GROUP TIME

REVIEW

Use the following Scripture passages and questions to discuss what you learned in your personal Bible study.

Recall the Big Idea for each of the five days of study.

Read Isaiah 36:1-22. Discuss the statements you starred on page 39. How can people fight with God's truth the lies the enemy tells?

Share about a time when you were waiting for God's rescue. Describe what your prayers were like, what you did, and what you might do differently after reading Hezekiah's story.

Talk about the way you filled in the PRAY acronym on page 46. What common themes show up in our group? How can we support one another as we try to build stronger, more patient prayer lives?

Share the decision you starred in the chart on page 49. Discuss answers to the question, How might taking a long-term mindset influence the choice you marked (p. 50)?

Draw an icon to represent the illustration that stood out most from God's promises in Isaiah 49:8-26. Explain why you chose that icon. (Hint: Review page 58.)

MEMORIZE

Read Isaiah 30:18 together as a group. Then, toss a beach ball to one girl in the group and ask her to recite the first few words. She passes the ball to another girl when she gets stuck. Keep going until the whole verse has been said.

WATCH

Use the fill-in-the-blanks and note-taking space as you watch the Session 3 teaching video together as a group.

What seems like the best timing to _____ with these things may not be the best timing to _____.

Realigning to God's _____ leads us to trust His _____.

It is the _____ ____ _____ and _____ that help us get off the wheel of worry.

Prayer is where the _____ meets the _____.

God _____ at just the right time.

God responds to humble _____.

What doesn't seem like a _____ can often be the most _____.

WOW: _____

WOE: _____

NOTES

PRAY

Help us, Lord, be present where we are, remembering the past and trusting You for the future.

TRUST *God's* COMFORT

SESSION FOUR

Trusting God's comfort when I'm exhausted, sad, or experiencing pain or crisis can be challenging. Instead, I want to numb and delay my discomfort. I don't feel like praying—I feel like watching TV and eating ice cream. These aren't inherently sinful comforts, but they don't offer the restorative comfort God longs to give us. Isaiah will help us discover that God extends His hand toward us. He doesn't crush us when we are weak; rather, He longs to renew our strength and walk with us through the trials and difficulties we face. He sent Jesus to bring us comfort and support in the moments we need it most. In the passages of Scripture we will study this week, Isaiah will teach us what it looks like to respond to God's offer of true comfort through deeper trust in Him.

MEMORY VERSE

But those who trust in the LORD will find new strength. They will soar high on wings like eagles. They will run and not grow weary. They will walk and not faint.

ISAIAH 40:31

BIG IDEA

When we trust in the Lord, He comforts us with new strength and energy.

Day One

COMFORT FOR THE WEARY

If you aren't familiar with the word *weary*, it means to be completely exhausted, worn-out, and to not have the strength to go any further.

When have you felt completely exhausted—physically, emotionally, mentally, or spiritually? What happened?

When I have tough days, all I want are my favorite creature comforts—watching TV, eating ice cream, changing into my comfy clothes, and checking out for the rest of the day. Today as we open the pages of Isaiah, we will find that trusting God's comfort includes discerning where to turn in our exhaustion. Sure, God gave us comfort foods. Hobbies can distract us from our exhaustion. Talking to a good friend can soothe us. The Lord can use these things to comfort us. But sometimes we comfort ourselves with methods of escape that aren't necessarily healthy. Isaiah often addressed God's desire to comfort His people. Today, we will explore what it looks like to trust God instead of our counterfeit comforts when we feel tired.

THE OFFER TO COMFORT

The prophecies found in Isaiah 40 were meant to encourage and comfort God's people during the Babylonian exile. His message addressed events that would happen more than 150 years after Isaiah's day.[1]

READ ISAIAH 40:1-11. What repeated word did God say over His people (v. 1)?

What illustration did Isaiah use to contrast the permanence of God's words (vv. 7-8)?

What profession did Isaiah use to describe how the Lord will care for His people (v. 11)?

I love the picture of the Lord leading the mother sheep with her young. He is the Shepherd feeding and caring tenderly for His flock. He has the "powerful arm" to strike (v. 10), but He uses that same arm to carry His lambs (v. 11). Isaiah revealed the Lord as a "strong and tender Shepherd-King."[2]

God's message of comfort wasn't only for those in Isaiah's day. In the middle of these comforting verses is a reminder that God's words aren't like withering grass or fading flowers. These words of God last forever—they apply to us today!

How have you experienced God's comfort through tender words or shepherding care when you had an exhausting season?

Shepherds provide, protect, and sometimes carry their lambs. God has been my Shepherd in seasons of grief, difficult circumstances, and spiritual fatigue. God longs to comfort us, but we must come to Him rather than seek to comfort ourselves.

THE AUTHORITY TO COMFORT

READ ISAIAH 40:12-26. Draw a line to the correct word to complete the sentences below:

Verse 12: God measured (and holds in His hands) . . .	the stars.
Verse 15: The nations of the world are like . . .	the circle of the earth.
Verses 18-19: God cannot be compared with . . .	a drop in a bucket, dust on a scale.
Verse 22: God sits above . . .	images and idols.
Verse 26: God created and knows by name . . .	the oceans (waters) and heavens.

Which of these descriptions of God's power and might stood out most to you?

Why do you think Isaiah took time to establish God's credibility?

Since God's people turned to counterfeit comforts, I wonder if Isaiah reminded them of God's position and power as the One to console them in their pain. He knows the name of every star (v. 26), and He knows your name as well. This same God longs to comfort you in your seasons of exhaustion and heartbreak. When you see God clearly, you can trust Him with your trials. He wants you to believe by faith that He is present and powerful in your pain.

READ ISAIAH 40:27-31. Underline in your Bible the questions the Lord asked Israel in verse 27.

The people brought God down to their level by thinking of Him as weary or forgetful. We can be in danger of doing the same thing, treating God as if He has human weaknesses. Many of us can relate to doubts about the Lord seeing or intervening during our times of distress—even if we wouldn't admit it out loud.

In your own words, describe the reminders about God's ability to care for His people found in verses 28-29.

When Isaiah used these questions, it was to remind them of God's character. Basically, he was saying, "Don't you know who your God really is?"

God is the everlasting Creator of the whole earth. He doesn't get exhausted like we do, and His understanding can't be measured. The Hebrew word for *weary* can be defined as "failure through loss of inherent strength," and the word *tired* as "pointing to exhaustion because of the hardness of life."[3] We can relate to these definitions in our own lives, but the Lord never loses strength or gets exhausted. Instead, He gives us power when we're weak.

THE BENEFITS OF COMFORT

In the last verse in this chapter, we find a conditional promise.

READ ISAIAH 40:31. Highlight the condition given to experience the benefits mentioned in this verse.

Depending on your translation you might have highlighted *trusting*, *waiting*, or *hoping*. These are different interpretations for the Hebrew word *qavah*, which means "to wait, look for, hope, expect."[4] If we are trusting, waiting, and hoping in the Lord, our counterfeit comforts will lose their shine. Waiting on the Lord isn't just sitting around doing nothing; it means living in a posture of hopeful expectation of His help.

What helps you trust, wait, and hope in the Lord when you're exhausted?

Isaiah showed it isn't duty but delight to trust God's comfort. When we understand that God longs to walk alongside us through the difficulties of life on a broken planet, we can take delight in simply walking this road with Him.

When we believe these truths wholeheartedly, we're inspired rather than guilted into trusting God more. When you have a weary day or season, I pray you will wait on the Lord to renew your strength. He knows all about the struggles, losses, and frustrations that lead to your exhaustion. And He calls you to wait on Him for the power and strength you'll never find in your own striving.

DAILY WRAP-UP

Today we focused on this truth: *When we trust in the Lord, He comforts us with new strength and energy.* How would you summarize your personal takeaway from today's study?

PRAYER

Lord, You are the everlasting God, the Creator of heaven and earth. I'm so glad You never grow tired of my constant need for Your strength. I get frustrated and weary often, and I need You. Help me to remember how big You are—especially in my moments of fatigue when I think temporary distractions are the answer. In Jesus's name, amen.

MEMORY VERSE ACTIVITY

Read Isaiah 40:31 aloud three times. You can find it printed on page 63.

Day Two

COMFORT IN HOLDING THE RIGHT HAND

BIG IDEA
God offers His
hand of help, but
we must turn away
from counterfeits to
receive His comfort.

Life can be scary, and our Creator knows it well. And when life gets scary, stressful, or makes us anxious, it's easy to reach for a quick fix—something to take our focus off our overwhelming situation and emotions. It might be scrolling through social media, enjoying comfort food, or watching the latest rom-com. Studies show that a chemical in our brain called dopamine gets released during enjoyable activities and plays a part in why people struggle with addiction. We are wired to repeat behaviors that bring us short-term pleasure.[5]

In today's passage, the Lord makes a case for choosing His help over counterfeit comforts. He wants us to reach for His hand rather than rely on fakes, which in the Bible were often idols. The idolatry of Isaiah's day included craftsmen making objects to be worshiped. We might read these passages with a sigh of relief because we don't physically bow before man-made statues. But idolatry didn't go out of style—it just looks a little different in modern culture.

"Just as God says here, 'I am he' (41:4), so Jesus said, 'I am he' (John 8:58; 18:5)."[6]

CONSIDER THE JUDGE

> **READ ISAIAH 41:1-7.** What legal language is in verse 1? What do we learn about God in these verses?

Isaiah prophesied about a conquering King who would come from "the east." But no matter who would come and what they would do, God is "the First and the Last" (v. 4)—He is always in control.

> Name a few things you are encouraged to know God is the First and Last (sovereign) over in the world and your own life.

As we see the Lord intervene in history, we remember that He is well aware of all that is happening in our world today. He is the First and Last—the blessed Controller of all things. Even when He allows discipline or difficulty, He offers His help and comfort.

Isaiah also predicted that the people of the world would strengthen their idols and encourage each other to be strong (vv. 6-7). God warned His own people not to hold hands with idols or even put their sole trust in each other to get them through the scary season of Persia's domination. Instead, He reminded them to reach for their Creator's hand.

CONSIDER HIS OFFER

> **READ ISAIAH 41:8-14.** Fill in the blanks with God's promises of help in the following verses. (Using the NLT Bible version helps with this exercise.)

Verse 9: "I have called you back from the ends of the earth."

I have _____.
I will not _____.

Verse 10: I am with _____.

I am your _____.
I will _____ you and _____ you.
I will hold you up with my _____
_____.

Verse 11: Anyone who opposes you will _____
_____.

Verse 13: I hold you by your right _____.
I am here to _____.

Verse 14: I will _____ you.
I am _____
_____.

"Since the phrase 'do not be afraid' is repeated so often in this section of the book, we know it is a central issue for the people in captivity. They are afraid God has abandoned them, so Isaiah reminds them again and again that this will not happen."[7]

"The word 'Redeemer' appears here in 41:14 for the first time in Isaiah, but it will appear thirteen more times between now and the end of the book."[8]

God knows our futures just as He knew the future for Isaiah's original audience. God called His people to hold His hand through the highs and lows of their circumstances. We must choose whether to hold hands with the things we can touch, taste, and feel or to reach out in faith to clasp God's outstretched arm.

CONSIDER THE POSSIBILITIES

READ ISAIAH 41:15-20. Fill in the chart completing "You will" and "I will" statements from the verses. One is filled in for you.

"YOU WILL"	"I WILL"
Verse 15	Verse 17
Verse 16	Verse 18
	Verse 19
	Verse 20 I will create/do this miracle.

How would you summarize the possibilities for those who choose to accept God's offer of help?

CONSIDER THE EVIDENCE

READ ISAIAH 41:21-29. Summarize the evidence against idols.

How does verse 24 define those who choose idols?

The Hebrew word in verse 24 used for "worthless" or "nothing" is *tow`ebah*, which means, "a disgusting thing, abomination, abominable."[9] Counterfeit comforts at best can't help and at worst offend our gracious God. When we let anything capture our hearts and imaginations more than Him, idolatry can creep into our lives.[10]

We all experience moments when we need a hand to hold. Perhaps we grieve a loss, fear the future, regret the past, or are just plain tired. In those times, we look for relief.

Identify some godly sources of comfort you have turned to in the past or could turn to moving forward.

God reaches out His hand, so we want to identify and pursue practices that position us to receive His help. Some godly comforts in my life include journaling, talking through problems with a friend, and sitting quietly with a hot cup of tea to reflect. Your list might look totally different. And remember, godly comforts don't have to be super spiritual. A hot bath, nap, or walk can relieve stress and help you rest in the Lord.

People and practices can help us in some moments, but only the Lord Himself can offer us the strength and help that brings lasting comfort. We need the Holy Spirit to help us consider the evidence as we ask ourselves whether we are reaching for fakes or the hand of the one true God who tells us:

MEMORY VERSE ACTIVITY
Read Isaiah 40:31 aloud one time. Then write it down in your book or on a separate piece of paper.

> For I hold you by your right hand—I, the LORD your God. And I say to you, "Don't be afraid. I am here to help you."
> ISAIAH 41:13

DAILY WRAP-UP

Today we focused on this truth: *God offers His hand of help, but we must turn away from counterfeits to receive His comfort.* How would you summarize your personal takeaway from today's study?

BIG IDEA
God doesn't
promise to remove
all difficulties in
our lives, but He
does comfort us
with His presence.

Day Three

COMFORT IN CRISIS

The seasons when trials are intense or long are described by Isaiah with metaphors like "deep waters," "rivers of difficulty," and "the fire of oppression" (Isa. 43:2). These aren't irritations—these are times when it feels like the ground is shaking beneath our feet.

Reflect on a time that felt like deep waters, rivers of difficulty, or fires of oppression in your life. Create a news headline to describe that time in your life. Keep that season in mind as you read the words of comfort God delivered through Isaiah.

Today's verses in Isaiah comfort us as we remember God doesn't remove all the difficulties in our lives, but He does comfort us with His presence.

COMFORT IN GOD'S PRESENCE

We jumped from Isaiah 41 to 43, but we will return to Isaiah 42 on Day Five to explore Jesus as our Source of comfort.

If possible, I'd love for you to read Isaiah 43:1-13 out loud. Then summarize the first five verses.

God created, formed, and ransomed you. He calls you by name and promises to be with you because He is your God (vv. 1-2). He says you are precious and loved, so you shouldn't be afraid (vv. 4-5). No one can snatch you out of His hand (v. 13).

This week our focus is on trusting God's comfort. The Hebrew word translated into our English word for *comfort* is *nacham*. It means "to be sorry, console oneself, repent, regret, comfort, be comforted."[11]

Which truth in the first part of Isaiah 43 is particularly comforting to you today, and why?

The Lord wouldn't abandon His people, but He would allow the discipline of exile. Their striving for idols and human comforts wouldn't deliver them. Eventually, their pain would help them see their need for the Lord and His deliverance. Isaiah's message pointed them to the identity of the One who would save them. God would be present in their trials, and He will be present in ours. We can trust His comfort even when our lives are turned upside down.

COMFORT IN GOD'S VICTORY

READ ISAIAH 43:14-28. What did the Lord promise to do for the exiles in Babylon (v. 14)?

What character qualities and displays of power in the past did God bring to their attention (vv. 15-17)?

What did the Lord tell them to do with the memories of the past, and why (vv. 18-19)?

What did the Lord say He would do with their sins (v. 25)?

These verses show us the priority of grace. The Lord didn't rescue His people because they were well-behaved. He comforted them because He is a faithful and forgiving God. That is good news for you and me because we also need rescue from our sin and struggles. A New Testament example of this same grace appears in Romans:

> But God showed his great love for us by sending
> Christ to die for us *while we were still sinners.*
> **ROMANS 5:8, EMPHASIS MINE**

The Lord also instructed His people to forget the past because He was doing a new thing. One commentator pointed out that God's fundamental principles don't change but His methods change with changing needs: "We are meant to reflect on the past with gratitude and stimulated faith but not to stereotype our expectations from God."[12] Last time God delivered through the waters of the Red Sea, and this time He would make a way through the desert.

Our God wants to do new things in our lives too! His principles don't change—His Word never fades, but His present deliverance might take a different shape than His rescue in the past. We can't expect the Lord to work according to a past formula because He is a God who does new things.

As you look back on your journey of faith, what are some things that have never changed?

Isaiah helps us glimpse God's gift of Himself and our responsibility to respond to His invitation. As we experience God's comfort, we can share it with others.

COMFORT TO SHARE

Read the following verse and circle the word *comfort(s)* each time you find it:

> He comforts us in all our troubles so that we can
> comfort others. When they are troubled, we will be
> able to give them the same comfort God has given us.
> **2 CORINTHIANS 1:4**

List some ways people have comforted you.

When people are going through "deep waters," "rivers of difficulty," or "the fire of oppression" (Isa. 43:2), we want to be sensitive in what we say and do. In difficult times, we want to avoid Christian clichés and learn from the model of God's comfort.

In Isaiah 43, we discovered God's comforting words:

- "I will be with you" in difficult times (v. 2).
- You are "precious," "honored," and "I love you" (v. 4).
- I "will blot out your sins" and "never think of them again" (v. 25).

These are words of comfort we can share with others in their pain.

> **Take a moment to think of someone you know who is going through deep waters. Write his or her name below and list some ideas for how you might comfort that person in a practical way.**

The Lord helps us through our difficulties with His love and presence, but He also calls us to share His comfort with others. The Israelites didn't ask for God's help, and they grew tired of Him. God called them to repent, but He didn't abandon them. Instead, He told them to forget the past and get ready for new things ahead. No matter what the past week, month, or year has held for us, we can start fresh today by receiving God's comfort and helping others do the same. Whether you are coming out of a trial, in the middle of the fire, or headed into the flames, hold onto the truth that the Lord loves you and is nearer than you think.

DAILY WRAP-UP

> **Today we focused on this truth: *God doesn't promise to remove all difficulties in our lives, but He does comfort us with His presence*. How would you summarize your personal takeaway from today's study?**

PRAYER

Lord, You know what I'm walking through right now. Comfort me so that I can comfort others for Your honor and glory. Help me know what to say and what not to say. Thank You for loving me, forgiving me, and assuring me that I won't drown in this river of difficulty! In Jesus's name, amen.

MEMORY VERSE ACTIVITY

Write down Isaiah 40:31. Also record one thought you have as you read over this verse.

BIG IDEA
God invites us
to come back to
Him when we've
gotten off course.

Day Four

COMFORT IN RETURNING TO GOD

Before we jump into today's study, let's take a moment to review what we've covered so far this week to help us trust in God's comfort rather than strive to soothe ourselves when life is hard. We've found:

- God's promise to comfort the weary (Isa. 40).
- God's offer of His right hand of help (Isa. 41).
- God's comfort during seasons of crisis (Isa. 43).

As you reflect on the first three days of study you completed this week, what truths stand out most in your mind regarding God's comfort?

Today's chapter in Isaiah adds an important element in our arsenal of truths regarding God's comfort. We can trust Him because He never stops calling us to come back to Him.

YOU BELONG TO GOD

READ ISAIAH 44:1-5. Record some hopeful truths that stand out to you.

One of the first things I noticed in these verses is that God tells His people not to fear (v. 2). This command, given so often in Scripture, reassures us that the Lord knows our tendency toward anxiety. He reminds us often that we don't have to be afraid because we can trust Him.

In verse 5, the Lord was speaking directly to the descendants of Israel, but He also spoke of future generations of people who would take the name of Israel as their own by writing God's name on their hands. For Isaiah's audience, this description would have brought to mind images of a servant being marked on the hand with the sign of their master.[13]

Reading this made me want to take out a marker and write "Yahweh" on my hand to mark myself as belonging to God! If we identify God as Master in our lives, we have marked our hands with His name spiritually, no Sharpie® required. We are some of the descendants God had in mind in verse 3. Whether we are of Jewish or Gentile descent, God invites us into a personal relationship with Him! The New Testament expands on this concept of belonging even more by showing us that through Jesus we move from God's servant to God's heir.

> **READ GALATIANS 4:4-7** in your Bible. Underline the benefits we
> receive as those who belong to God.

We are more than just servants. Through Christ we are children who receive a spiritual inheritance of eternal life. Our sin can guilt us into feeling like we aren't the sons and daughters of God or don't deserve to be. But the same God who spoke these words to idol-worshiping, forgetful Israel is the God who speaks them to us today. These truths from Isaiah 44 and Galatians 4 bring us comfort and hope when we don't feel like we belong anywhere.

> Based on these verses, how does God respond to repentant sinners
> who humbly come back to Him?

> How have you personally experienced God's grace when you have
> returned to Him on the other side of a wandering season?

Whether we've gotten off course for a short or long period of time, the Lord welcomes us back into relationship when we return. He comforts us with the promise of restoration but also warns us of the consequences of counterfeits.

THE FUTILITY OF COUNTERFEIT GODS

We've seen the Lord consistently plead His case against idolatry throughout this week. Here is a brief look at the progression we've seen:

- Idols aren't able to explain the meaning of the past or tell the future (41:21-29).

- Idols aren't able to save their people or keep the Lord from saving them (43:8-13).

- Idols aren't able to predict the future or save their worshipers from it (44:7-8).

READ ISAIAH 44:6-20. Summarize in a few statements why God says idols are foolish.

The Lord says the idol-maker never stops to reflect that he is literally making his own god (v. 19). Without deeper reflection, we can fall into the same trap. One of the ways the Lord calls us to come back to Him is by reminding us to think deeply about the counterfeits we hold in our hands.

We may not carve our idols out of wood, but when we turn to comforts that provide short-term release and long-term regret, God calls us to reflect. What we have in our hearts ultimately ends up in our hands. Is the thing we are holding in our hands, thinking about in our minds, watching with our eyes, or shoving in our mouths really going to satisfy? We must consider whether our creature comforts can actually deliver. God invites us to return to Him even if the last five times we turned toward counterfeits. We are never past the point of coming back to Him.

THE CALL TO RETURN

The Hebrew word for *return* is *shuwb* and two definitions for this word used more than nine hundred times in the Old Testament include "to return, turn back" and "to reverse, revoke."[14]

READ ISAIAH 44:21-28. Write out verse 22 below, putting the word "RETURN" in all caps.

We find comfort in God's call to come back to Him again and again. It is possible for us to return to Him because of His faithfulness to redeem us rather than our good behavior. The Hebrew word in verse 22 is *ga'al*. This is the same word used of a kinsman redeemer in Jewish culture, a close relative who could restore property and honor to those who had lost it (Ruth 2:20). *Ga'al* means "to redeem, act as kinsman-redeemer, avenge, revenge, ransom."[15] We can return to God because He has chosen to pay the price for our sins through a promised Messiah.

What actions did Isaiah suggest based on the Lord's redemption (v. 23)?

Singing and shouting celebrated the good news that we don't have to stay on the wrong path. We can return to God as many times as we need to because He has paid the price for our sins.

What would it look like for you to answer God's invitation to return to Him in your present season?

We want to move toward God, but we don't always know what first steps to take. Here are some ideas to consider after wandering down the path of wrong thoughts, attitudes, or actions:

- Choose to reconnect with a friend who builds you up spiritually and speaks biblical truth into your life.
- Memorize Scriptures that especially speak to your current struggles.
- Remove apps from your phone that distract you from wholehearted devotion to God.
- Write prayer requests on slips of paper and put them in a mason jar. Pray over a few each day.
- Go for a prayer walk outside while confessing sin and asking God for direction.

These ideas are not a prescriptive checklist to approach with a striving posture. Coming back to the Lord might mean you stop doing something that is not good for you, or it might mean pressing into practices like praying, studying God's Word, or attending church. Returning is ultimately about a change of direction in your mind and will.

In modern Christian circles, we often talk about turning our hearts toward God. The Hebrew understanding of the heart wasn't about feelings. Instead, the heart referred to

PRAYER

Lord, it's so good to remember that You have redeemed me! I belong to You. Your name may not be written on my hand physically, but it is written on my heart. When I get lost on the road toward sin, show me the way back to You. Thank You for Isaiah's words that reveal You as First and Last, Creator, and Redeemer. I believe today that You are who You say You are! In Jesus's name, amen.

MEMORY VERSE ACTIVITY

Attempt to write out Isaiah 40:31 from memory. Then check to see how you did.

the mind and the will. Think about it as turning around if you've been running from the Lord with your choices and deciding instead to head toward Him with both your mind and your will. He is waiting for you.

He calls us back . . .

- Even when we've messed up again and again;
- Even when we repeat the same mistake;
- Even when we've said we're "sorry and want to change" a hundred times before.

God never considers us too far gone. In His grace He offers us freedom from our sin patterns and empowers us to pursue holiness, but we will never stop sinning completely this side of heaven. That means we must make a habit of coming back to God again and again for forgiveness and comfort.

In our study of Isaiah's message, we have read the words of a prophet committed to God. But his response in God's presence was, "It's all over! I am doomed," and he referred to himself as a man of unclean lips (Isa. 6:5). Isaiah messed up just like you and I do. Even as God's prophetic mouthpiece, Isaiah knew he didn't always say and do the right things. But the Lord continued to use him despite his imperfections.

The many Messianic references in Isaiah point to the future sacrifice of Jesus as the pathway to redemption, the way we return to our holy God in our struggle with sin. Whether our sin falls into the category of small mistakes or major mess-ups, we have a Redeemer who has paid the price to set us free. He made us and will not forget us. Just as the Lord continued to work in Isaiah's life, He is always working in us too—conforming us more and more to the image of His Son.

DAILY WRAP-UP

Today we focused on this truth: *God invites us to come back to Him when we've gotten off course.* How would you summarize your personal takeaway from today's study?

Day Five

COMFORT IN CHRIST

Can you think of a season of suffering in your life when you found comfort from those who had walked a similar path?

SCRIPTURE
FOCUS
Isaiah 42

BIG IDEA
Christ offers comfort
as the Servant
who understands
suffering.

While none of our grief looks exactly like another's, we can find comfort alongside those who have similar circumstances. When someone can say, "I know this kind of pain," it normalizes our suffering so we don't feel totally alone. And today we will discover One who can truly comfort each of us. No matter the source of our suffering, Jesus came to strengthen and support us. He set us free in a way no one else could because His suffering accomplished a restored relationship with our Creator. He would bring light and liberty to the world according to Isaiah's revelation of the Suffering Servant.

CHRIST'S SUFFERING

We've seen "servant" language in other places in Isaiah that often referred to the nation of Israel as God's servant. In those passages the servant is fearful and blind although loved by the Lord. God used this servant to reveal Himself to the nations. In contrast, the Servant Songs (Isa. 42:1-4; 49:1-6; 50:4-11; and 52:13–53:12) portray a Messiah who is always obedient to God and whose mission is to bring light and justice to the nations.[16] This Servant would bring hope and comfort.

> **READ ISAIAH 42:1-9.** Record what stands out to you about the Lord's chosen servant.

The Lord told His people the future before it would happen. Remember these words were written approximately seven hundred years before Christ's birth.

Thinking about what you know of Jesus from the New Testament, how do you see Him as the fulfillment of this Messianic prophecy?

We may all have different answers, but some things I considered include:

- How the Holy Spirit descended on Jesus when He was baptized (Matt. 3:16);
- How Jesus approached a woman broken in sin. He didn't crush her but called her to repent (John 8:1-11);
- How Jesus healed a blind man (John 9:1-7);
- How I was a slave to sin, and Jesus set me free with the power to obey Him.

Now let's turn to a New Testament passage that puts to rest any doubt that these prophecies in Isaiah 42 refer to Jesus.

READ MATTHEW 12:15-21. Note what Jesus was doing just before Isaiah's words were quoted.

Unger's Bible Dictionary defines the "bruised reed" in Isaiah 42:3 as those who are: "spiritually miserable and helpless."[17]

Jesus was healing the sick. He had compassion for those who were suffering. He understands that we are people who often feel like a bruised reed or a candle on the verge of burnout. We can find others to comfort us when we experience brokenness and weariness, but only Jesus can ultimately bring the kind of healing we need. Jesus understands our pain personally. We can find comfort in His love and realize that following Him sometimes means following a path of suffering.

SUFFERING WITH CHRIST

Read the verses below and underline the words *suffer* or *suffering* as you encounter them:

> And since we are his children, we are his heirs. In fact, together with Christ we are heirs of God's glory. But if we are to share his glory, we must also share his suffering.
> **ROMANS 8:17**

> I want to know Christ and experience the
> mighty power that raised him from the dead.
> I want to suffer with him, sharing in his death.
> **PHILIPPIANS 3:10**

> Instead, be very glad—for these trials make you partners with Christ in his suffering, so that you will have the wonderful joy of seeing his glory when it is revealed to all the world.
> **1 PETER 4:13**

Since our Messiah was prophesied to be a Suffering Servant, I wonder why I'm always relatively shocked at the sting of suffering in my own life. My son recently updated his prayer requests with our family in an app we use on our phones to pray for one another. He wrote several requests but the last one read,

> "Pray that I would process through these questions:
> 1. What does it look like for me to suffer for Christ in my life?
> 2. Where am I running away from suffering for Christ?
> 3. How can I actively love others by putting their needs first in my life?"

He added a note that he doesn't want suffering for suffering's sake. Instead, he wants to adjust his view to align with biblical suffering. I share this because I believe a realignment to a biblical view of suffering is needed in my life and maybe in yours as well.

Take a moment to apply my son's three prayer questions to your life. In the space below or on a separate piece of paper, jot down any ideas or thoughts in response to each question from above.

Jesus knows you will suffer—sometimes because you live on a broken planet, other times as a result of your own poor choices, and maybe even because you are a Christ-follower. When you suffer, you can hold onto these truths: Jesus understands pain. Jesus won't crush you in times of brokenness. Jesus came to bring you freedom through His suffering.

We can trust in God's comfort because He sent Jesus as His Servant on our behalf. Our suffering doesn't mean the Lord doesn't love us. Instead of striving to avoid suffering, we can stir our affections for Jesus. He can use the good and the bad in our lives to draw us nearer to Him. For the people in Isaiah's day, the Lord told them way ahead of time that He would send a Servant to save them. We are privileged to know His name is Jesus and benefit from a more developed picture of who God's Servant is as He has been revealed to us in Scripture.

READ PHILIPPIANS 2:6-8. God elevated Jesus to the place of highest honor after He fulfilled His humble service. How is the Lord calling you to take the attitude of Christ in your current challenges?

To end today, READ ISAIAH 42:10-17. Then, either write your own words of praise to the Lord or write Isaiah 42:12 as your personal heart-cry.

Finding others who share our struggles can be helpful, but it is good to know we all have access to Jesus. You can sing even on dark days because Jesus is the Servant of the Lord who will not crush you; He will free you! He fulfilled the words of Isaiah as the Messianic Servant who comforts the broken. His name is the hope of the nations and our personal hope when we feel bruised and burnt out. Let this truth sink deep and bring you comfort today.

DAILY WRAP-UP

Today we focused on this truth: *Christ offers comfort as the Servant who understands suffering.* How would you summarize your personal takeaway from today's study?

MEMORY VERSE ACTIVITY

Write out or say aloud Isaiah 40:31 from memory.

Session Four
GROUP TIME

REVIEW
Use the following Scripture passages and questions to discuss what you learned in your personal Bible study.

Recall the Big Idea for each of the five days of study. Identify the one that stood out to you most.

Describe your go-to creature comfort when you're exhausted.

Read Isaiah 41:1-7. Name reasons it's encouraging to know God is the First and the Last (sovereign). (For help, see page 68.)

Discuss how choosing to accept God's offer of help can help us in tough times.

Come up with names of people in your church going through deep waters. Brainstorm practical ways our group could help. Refer to page 75 for ideas.

Talk about answers to the question, What would it look like for you to answer God's invitation to return to Him (p. 79)? Then discuss the ideas you'd like to implement from the list provided.

Read Isaiah 42:10-17. Share your own words of praise from page 84 or lyrics from a favorite praise song that speak the same message.

MEMORIZE
As you read Isaiah 40:31 aloud, invite girls to stand and act out the verse.

WATCH

Use the fill-in-the-blanks and note-taking space as you watch the Session 4
teaching video together as a group.

Where we look for comfort will either _____
us or _____ us spiritually.

At best, the ways we strive for comfort are an _____
or a _____.

What does it really look like to receive God's _____?

To _____ through it, we have to ____ through it.

These _____ might be keeping us from the _____
_____ of our heart.

We can't be _____ about _____.

Your soul will _____ to the _____ of the pleasures you pursue.

Idols give us an _____ with comfort without a
connection to the _____.

WOW: _____

WOE: _____

NOTES

PRAY

Heavenly Father, help us see how You have comforted Your people throughout history and
provided the ultimate comfort to us in Jesus.

TRUST *God's* COMMANDS

SESSION FIVE

Trusting God's commands in a world that tells us to follow our feelings can be challenging. He longs to give us the peace that comes with doing things His way, but we wander off His path over and over. This week we will look at several truths from Isaiah that help us understand why God's commands matter and the consequences of failing to obey them. The amazing truth is God knows we can't obey Him perfectly because of our sin nature, so He promised to send a Messiah to save us. Right living is possible only through Jesus's incredible sacrifice. Let's sit at Isaiah's feet this week and listen for the Holy Spirit to address any areas where we can grow in trusting God's commands.

Who among you fears the LORD and obeys his servant?
If you are walking in darkness, without a ray of light, trust in the LORD and rely on your God.

ISAIAH 50:10

SCRIPTURE FOCUS

Isaiah 48

BIG IDEA

God calls us to listen and obey His commands that lead to peace.

Day One

COMMANDS THAT LEAD TO PEACE

As we begin our next two weeks of study in Isaiah with a focus on trusting God's commands and correction, we want to be sure we hold onto God's character and heart behind His instructions. We'll also need to identify places where our own filter of experience might skew our understanding.

> How might other authorities or experiences in your life (past or present) affect the way you approach God's commands in the Bible?

People are all imperfect and may punish unfairly or not obey the standards they set for others. But God's instructions are not tainted by a human sin nature. We want to be careful not to transfer the behavior of imperfect human authorities onto Him. In Isaiah's message, we will find that God's commands invite us closer rather than push us further from Him and we will learn how obedience leads to peace.

OUR DISOBEDIENCE PROBLEM

Last week when we left God's people, Isaiah's message predicted their exile in Babylon. Isaiah 48 reveals prophetic messages regarding their return to their homeland from their captivity.

> **READ ISAIAH 48:1-11.** Highlight in your Bible the one word command repeated in verse 1.

> List the words the Lord used to describe the people living in exile (vv. 4,8).

Why did the Lord say He would hold back His anger (vv. 9,11)?

Rebellion isn't about disobeying because you don't know the rules; it's choosing to disobey even when you know they rules.[1]

In many passages of Scripture, we read about people with a habit of turning away from their Maker. Our sin nature doesn't direct us toward obedience. All of us struggle to stay within the boundaries God provides. Our problem with rebellion started in the garden of Eden when Adam and Eve ate from the tree God marked as "off limits" and we continue to struggle with it today.

Fill in the blanks to identify one command that is clear in Scripture that you struggle to obey:

_____ [your name] often struggles with God's command to _____.

To grow in trusting God's commands, we must acknowledge our propensity to ignore them. We need the Lord's help—His Word, His Spirit, His community—to support us in our pursuit of obedience. We can't comply on our own. And even when we get off course, the Lord doesn't turn away. Instead, He disciplines us like a loving Father and charts a course back to Him.

LISTEN AND OBEY

The very first word of chapter 48 includes the command to "hear" or "listen." In Hebrew this word is *shama*, which doesn't just mean to understand facts; it also implies obedience to what is heard.[2] This same word is found ten times in chapter 48.[3] When God repeats a word that many times in one chapter, we want to take notice. God doesn't delight in correction, so He encourages us to listen to and obey His commands.

READ ISAIAH 48:12-22. Fill in the chart below in your own words.

WHAT WE LEARN ABOUT GOD	WHAT HE COMMANDS US TO DO	WHAT HE WANTS FOR US
Verse 12	Verse 12	Verse 17
Verse 13	Verse 14	Verse 18
Verse 16 He predicted the future. He is Sovereign and His Spirit gives messages.	Verse 16	Verse 19 Descendants not destruction
Verse 17	Verse 20 Be free, sing and shout.	Verse 20

God calls us to come together and come close. He wants a deep relationship with us that only happens as He reveals Himself to us. Through this revelation, we can worship and obey Him with understanding. We can trust His commands because they reveal the way God created people to live.

Take a few moments now to sit quietly before the Lord. Ask Him to reveal any areas in your life that need attention as you think about your choices and His commands. Then jot down any areas where you want to follow the Lord more closely.

We learned in our first week of study that God is holy, which means set apart. As 1 Peter 1:16 says, "For the Scriptures say, 'You must be holy because I am holy.'" While God gives us grace in our failures, He also empowers us through His Spirit to live holy lives. We don't have to walk down the path of sin because God offers us "everything we need for living a godly life" (2 Pet. 1:3).

BLESSINGS ACCOMPANY OBEDIENCE

We won't ever be perfect this side of heaven, but we can grow in obedience to God's commands. And when we listen, God showers us with blessings. God is always faithful, but some blessings are only given when we obey. This doesn't mean you'll have health, wealth, and constant happiness if you obey God, though.

> **Look back at Isaiah 48:18,22. Jot down the blessing God wants to give to the righteous but withholds from the wicked.**

The blessings God offers those who listen aren't circumstantial ease or material blessings. God's commands lead to life and freedom, and one of the side effects on this path is peace. We can't listen to and obey God to manipulate Him into granting us peace. Rather, we recognize that trusting God's commands with our obedience leads to a life of peace.

Some of the most miserable times in my life have included seasons when I've been actively walking in sin. Those seasons are devoid of peace. All the worldly pursuits that promise peace don't deliver in the end. God said it clearly through the prophet Isaiah: "there is no peace for the wicked" (v. 22).

> **On a scale of 1 to 10, where is your peace level right now? I'm not asking about peaceful or chaotic circumstances. I mean how is the stillness in your soul?**
>
> 1   2   3   4   5   6   7   8   9   10
>
> No peace   Lots of peace
>
> **How might striving less and trusting God more give you more peace this week?**

In today's passage, God encouraged His people to trust His command to do something that would seem impossible to them—leave captivity in Babylon. Isaiah reminded the people that if God could make water spring from a rock (v. 21), then He could handle bringing them back from Babylon. God offers supernatural power to help us, but He also calls us to active trust that shows itself in our behaviors.

DAILY WRAP-UP

Today we focused on this truth: *God calls us to listen and obey His commands that lead to peace.* How would you summarize your personal takeaway from today's study?

Day Two

INSPIRED TO OBEY

I knew something was off. I couldn't state any particular sin or wrongdoing, but I didn't feel good about the growing exclusivity among my friends. I noticed conversations crossing the line into gossip more and more frequently. After months of neglecting to address these issues directly, a huge blow-up occurred with these same friends and ended over a decade of relationships. My choices to participate in gossip didn't bring consequences right away. But eventually, the pain came to the gossipers and their victims—I found myself in both categories.

Isaiah's message reveals that even when we don't immediately experience painful effects, sin is serious. The nation of Israel rebelled by chasing other gods over several years. They likely thought they were getting away with it, but Isaiah warned that they would experience discipline firsthand through an exile in Babylon.

SIN AND SUFFERING

> **READ ISAIAH 50:1-3.** What did the Lord say was the cause of His people's suffering?

Two different words were used to describe the true reason for the people's suffering in verse 1. The first is the Hebrew word *awon,* which one scholar defined as "inner perversion of the heart." The second is *pesha*, or "willful rebellion."[4] Bible translators have used a variety of English words in an attempt to capture the Hebrew meanings:

- "Wrongdoings . . . wrongful acts" (NASB);
- "Sins . . . sins" (NLT);
- "Sins . . . transgressions" (NIV);
- "Iniquities . . . transgressions" (CSB, ESV).

These words hit close to home for us. After studying this passage yesterday, I found myself tempted to compromise one of my own personal values. I was having that internal dialogue justifying why it would be OK to make a small concession when the Holy Spirit brought to my mind the seriousness of sin in today's passage. When I focused on the truth that even little compromises affect my own soul and invite divine discipline, the decision to say "no" to sin was a little easier. That is my prayer for us today—that knowing the suffering associated with sin will keep us from making it a habit.

> Write out a brief prayer asking the Lord to help you pursue right living and turn away from sin in your life.

We may know sin causes suffering, but that alone isn't enough to keep us away from it. We need divine help to obey God's commands.

IMITATING THE SERVANT

Right after Isaiah spoke about iniquities and transgressions causing pain, He recorded another Servant Song. Remember there are four poems in Isaiah foretelling the Messiah as a Servant. After the Lord reaffirmed sin as the cause of His people's exile, we find a poem to remind us that God's Servant Jesus is the ultimate answer to our sin situation.

> **READ ISAIAH 50:4-11.** Write what the "Sovereign LORD" (NLT, NIV) or "Lord GOD" (CSB, ESV, NASB) did for the Servant (Jesus) in the following verses:

> Verse 4:

> Verse 5:

> Verse 7:

> Verse 9:

Sin is serious, but these verses remind us that striving against sin won't free us from its entanglement. Christ, the Servant, delivers God's people from sin. God knows we can't overcome sin without His help. He is on our side in the battle against sin! Four times in this passage the Servant used the name *Adonai Yahweh*—"Sovereign LORD" (NLT, NIV) or "Lord GOD" (CSB, ESV, NASB). By using the name *Adonai* (Master, My Lord) and *Yahweh* (the personal name for God) together, we see an emphasis on God's role as a master to be obeyed who also longs to have a personal relationship with us. I want us to see the New Testament connections with Isaiah 50:6 firsthand.

> **Read the following verses and underline in your Bible any sections that relate to Isaiah's mention of the Messiah being beaten, mocked, or spat upon:**
>
> - Matthew 26:67
> - Matthew 27:30
> - Mark 15:19
> - Luke 22:63-65

The Servant obeyed the Lord fully but still suffered, and we know His pain didn't end with beating, mockery, and spitting. He died a criminal's death on the cross. Jesus said if we want to follow Him, then we must deny ourselves and take up our own cross (Matt. 16:24). He isn't asking us to literally die, but to choose to die to our own desires and sins so we can live for Him.

If we believe this, our faith can't be a hobby or side-gig. It takes over our entire lives—our words, attitudes, and actions are shaped by God's Word on every subject. We stop trusting our own definitions or expectations of what is right and wrong and submit to His. When we follow the Servant, we are inspired to imitate Him.

> **How does Jesus's commitment to the Father's will (and our salvation) inspire you to imitate Him?**

RELIANCE ON GOD

> **Write out our memory verse this week, Isaiah 50:10.**

*Lord, thank You
for reminding me
of sin's serious
consequences.
I want to turn from
sin and turn toward
You. Thank You for
sending Jesus to
rescue me from
sin. I want to trust
You more. Help
me rely on You by
pressing into our
relationship, totally
focused on loving
You. Give me the
discernment to see
Your heart behind
Your instructions. In
Jesus's name, amen.*

Isaiah used two different words to emphasize what those who fear the Lord and want to obey His Servant must do—trust and rely. The Hebrew word for "trust" is *batach*, which means "to trust in, to have confidence, be confident, to be bold, to be secure."[5] To "rely" is *sha'an* and means "to lean on, trust in, support."[6] To find light in our darkness, we can lean into the Lord and put our confidence in Him as our place of safety.

These two words line up well with our overall theme in Isaiah of striving less and trusting God more. Right on the heels of the call to trust and rely on God comes a strong warning against living in our own light and warming ourselves by our own fires. God's response to our self-reliance has the same consequences as sin. Making idols out of people, work, material goods, self-sufficiency, or anything but the Lord will ultimately bring suffering.

> **How is the Lord calling you away from striving on your own and toward relying on Him?**

In a world full of blurred lines, the Lord calls us to humbly trust Him and His righteousness. We can do this when we make His Servant, Jesus, our safe place and press into Him with confidence.

DAILY WRAP-UP

> Today we focused on this truth: *The contrast between the sins of God's people and the obedience of God's Servant inspires us to pursue obedience.* How would you summarize your personal takeaway from today's study?

MEMORY VERSE ACTIVITY
Read Isaiah 50:10 aloud one time. Then write it down in your book or on a separate piece of paper.

Day Three

THE DISTINCTION OF LIPS AND HEARTS

SCRIPTURE FOCUS

Isaiah 29; 30

Israel built a temple, made sacrifices, and gathered for worship with the initial goal of authentic relationship with their personal God. They understood His holiness, His requirements, and His mercy through atonement. Their animal sacrifices were designed by God to foreshadow the ultimate sacrifice—Jesus dying to restore intimacy between a sinful people and a holy God. Over time, though, many of their spiritual practices drifted from heartfelt expressions to religious checklists. They began to trust the rituals of their faith rather than God.

BIG IDEA

Trusting God's commands isn't just about external compliance but internal transformation.

We can find ourselves in this same struggle. We may have started reading our Bibles, praying, or going to church out of love for the Lord. But over time we can drift when we lose sight of our "why." God calls us to make sure that what's in our minds makes it to our hearts too. Israel's rebellion was an outward symptom of the deeper issue of wayward hearts. The words of Isaiah we will examine today reveal to us that trusting God's commands goes beyond just saying or doing the right thing (giving Him lip service) to being transformed on the inside too (letting Him change our hearts).

THE PROBLEM WITH HYPOCRISY

Chapters 28–35 in Isaiah are sometimes labeled the "woe" oracles because of the repetition of the Hebrew word *hoy* ("woe"), warning of actions that displease the Lord.[7] Much of God's displeasure is related to His people's idolatry and hypocrisy.

READ ISAIAH 29:1-4,13-16. Summarize God's charges in your own words.

From these verses, it seems as though Jerusalem claimed immunity from God's judgment based on their sacrifices and worship. The Lord made clear He was not pleased with worship and obedience that didn't come from the heart. We must guard against going through the motions of worship when our hearts and daily actions are far from God. God doesn't want empty or hypocritical ceremonies. He gave rituals to reinforce—not replace—spiritual truth.

As you think about your acts of worship and obedience, where does it feel like you're going through the motions spiritually?

How often are you expecting encounters with God in worship with your church or on your own?

During His earthly ministry, Jesus encountered people who needed to hear Isaiah's words about heartfelt worship. Some Pharisees (major rule-followers) criticized Jesus for not mandating that His disciples perform traditional hand-washing procedures. Jesus quoted Isaiah in correcting their logic.

READ MATTHEW 15:7-9 in your Bible. Circle the words *hearts* and *lips* when you read them.

The Pharisees were known for heaping on extra rules. As we study God's commands this week, we aren't looking to compound any guilt we already experience in our struggles. Instead, any guilt is removed when we learn to trust God and obey Him from the heart.

WORSHIP FROM THE HEART

Judgment is very much a part of Isaiah's message, but it is not the final word. Hope is the final word. God calls His people to know Him, trust Him, and love Him. When they choose to walk in rebellion, He disciplines them to help them realize what they are missing—real relationship with their Creator. His temporary judgment can lead to permanent hope when His people trade religious routines for personal intimacy with God.

READ ISAIAH 29:5-8,17-24. List two or three hopeful things the future holds for God's people.

Look again at verse 23. Rather than checklists or personal pride, what is the motivation for genuine worship?

Trusting God's commands isn't about checking off a list of rules we've obeyed or changing what we do, it's about allowing God to transform us from the inside out as we fall more in love with Him. Our God is the Holy One, and we are His creation. Above all, we were created to glorify Him. As we understand who He is and who we are in Christ, we can worship from the heart.

READ ISAIAH 30:15,18-22. Summarize God's message in verse 15.

List some specific ways you can trust God more in your acts of worship and obedience—prayer, Bible study, church attendance, and so on.

For me to return, rest, ask, and wait for the Lord, I've realized I must create space for these types of activities in my busy life: reflecting, taking quiet walks, praying, journaling, active listening, reading God's Word, intentionally releasing worries, and limiting technology. We try so hard to figure out next steps by striving more when Scripture shows that the Lord speaks most often in the quiet. He promises to teach us and guide us. Isaiah 30:21 says when we ask for help and then wait patiently for Him, He will tell us where to go.

Lord, I want to worship You with my mouth and my heart. Change me from the inside out. My behavior needs to change, but help me to trust Your commands in returning, reflecting, and in quiet pursuit of You! In Jesus's name, amen.

MEMORY VERSE ACTIVITY

Write down Isaiah 50:10. Also record one thought you have as you read over this verse.

When we shift our focus from ourselves to God, we show Him that we believe He is enough and we trust Him with our details.

> Circle one of the ideas from your list of ways you can trust God more in your acts of worship and obedience. When will you make space to try this idea? (For example, "When I first wake up, I'll take three minutes to journal a prayer about my hopes for the day.")

Today's popular messages encourage us to just believe in ourselves. They tell us to do what we want, believe what we want, and live how we want. The resounding call of "you do you" parallels the postures that brought judgment for the nation of Judah. But we want to trust God's commands so we don't put our confidence in the wrong places, like empty religious motions and our ability to save ourselves. By pursuing intimacy with God, we can stay connected to His heart behind the commands. We don't want to engage in worthless worship, so we seek God's help to align our lips and hearts.

DAILY WRAP-UP

> Today we focused on this truth: *Trusting God's commands isn't just about external compliance but internal transformation.* How would you summarize your personal takeaway from today's study?

Day Four

INSTRUCTIONS FIRST

The Lord He has clearly communicated His standards. As we seek to trust God's commands, we want to lean into the importance of seeking His heart behind His instructions. Let's read today's passages curiously knowing the Lord gave these warnings about sin so His people would know what pleases Him and what doesn't.

BIG IDEA
God clearly communicates His commands so we will understand His expectations.

BLESSINGS FOR OBEDIENCE

READ ISAIAH 58. Circle the best answer:

How did the people's fasting displease God (vv. 3-4)?

A. They did it to please themselves.
B. They oppressed their workers while fasting.
C. They kept on fighting and quarreling.
D. All of the above.

What other commands did the Lord give (vv. 9-10)?

A. Stop spreading rumors.
B. Remove the heavy yoke of oppression.
C. Feed the hungry and help those in trouble.
D. All of the above.

What commandment did God instruct the people to observe carefully (vv. 13-14)?

A. Work harder.
B. Honor the Sabbath.
C. Judge others.
D. All of the above.

As you consider these commands given through the prophet Isaiah, highlight the ones that are still important for Christians to obey today.

Answers: D, D, B

These commands are still important for us today, they just look different in practice. When it comes to keeping the Sabbath, Jesus didn't cancel God's call to rest, but He did fulfill the law and become our place of spiritual rest (Matt. 12). Fasting is still an important spiritual discipline, as long as people fast with humble hearts to draw near to the Lord, not to please themselves and "feel" spiritual. Trusting God's commands means knowing them and asking for His help to understand how to live them out today.

List some practical ways you can live out God's commands in each of these areas.

• **Sharing food, shelter, and clothing with those in need (Isa. 58:7,10):**

• **Refraining from gossip and spreading rumors (v. 9):**

• **Prioritizing rest as a regular spiritual practice (v. 13):**

Which one of these commands needs the most attention in your own life?

Before we move on to chapter 59, I don't want us to miss the blessings the Lord wants to give those who trust His commands. As we read in Isaiah 58, fill in the blanks to list the blessings those who obey the Lord would experience:

- Salvation coming like _____ _____ (v. 8);

- Wounds healing _____ (v. 8);

- _____ leading them forward (v. 8);

- God's _____ protecting them from behind (v. 8);

- The Lord answering their call with, "Yes, ___ _____ _____" (v. 9);

- Their _____ shining out from the _____ (v. 10);

- The Lord _____ them continually and _____ their strength (v. 11);

- Flourishing like a well-watered _____ (v. 11);

- Returning to their homeland as a _____ and _____ (v. 12);

- The Lord honoring them and satisfying them with His promised _____ (v. 14).

What stands out to you as you read through this list of blessings?

Not only does the Lord warn us about His expectations before bringing consequences, He also gives us an opportunity to turn back to Him and receive incredible blessings.

CONSEQUENCES FOR DISOBEDIENCE

READ ISAIAH 59:1-8. Summarize God's message about sin in this passage.

Several times in today's passages we encountered the themes of light and darkness. Isaiah reminds us that aligning our lives with God's truth will lead us to light in a dark world. Running on the path toward sin will only take us further into the darkness.

Isaiah said sin starts in people's minds and then action follows (v. 4). The world loves to disguise sin as shiny and fun, but the Lord says it leads to danger and bondage. Isaiah used the metaphors of "deadly snakes" and "spiders' webs" to illustrate this principle (v. 5). He also said the people had "mapped out crooked roads, and no one who follows them knows a moment's peace" (Isa. 59:8). The road to sin doesn't lead to peace but instead to suffering and entrapment.

READ ISAIAH 59:9-21. What illustrations were used to describe sinners in verses 9-11?

What things did Isaiah say were gone according to verses 14-15?

What did the Lord do since no one helped the oppressed (vv. 16-17)?

Who would the Redeemer come to save (v. 20)?

What would the Lord give that would never leave them (v. 21)?

Look at the good news Isaiah delivered! The Lord would step in and redeem His people by sending a Redeemer, who we know to be His Son, Jesus. This Redeemer would restore sinful people back to Him. He would also give His Spirit and His Word to sanctify them in their daily battle with sin.

We can't claim that we don't know God's commands or excuse ourselves by stating our confusion over which rules to obey. Doing that reveals our immaturity rather than our desire to strive less and trust God more. Instead, we want to press into God's truth, discern His directions, and embrace the blessings and peace obedience brings.

DAILY WRAP-UP

Today we focused on this truth: *God clearly communicates His commands so we will understand His expectations.* How would you summarize your personal takeaway from today's study?

PRAYER

Lord, help us know how to apply Your commands in our lives today. When we veer from Your truth, realign our hearts to Yours. We want to obey Your instructions rather than justify and excuse behaviors that don't please You. Show us where we've walked the path toward sin so we can return to the path of peace. In Jesus's name, amen.

MEMORY VERSE ACTIVITY

Attempt to write out Isaiah 50:10 from memory, then check to see how you did.

Day Five

RIGHTEOUSNESS IN CHRIST

Sometimes when we study God's commands, we can feel overwhelmed by how easy it is to get off track. Though we might desire to fully obey the Lord, we lack the ability to follow through in all areas. This can leave us discouraged as we think about our position before a holy God. Thankfully, our God knows we can't become righteous through our own efforts. Although today's chapters contain some heavy truths, they also encourage us as we read about God's plan to free us from the penalty of sin. My prayer as you study today is that Isaiah's prophecies about Christ, the Suffering Servant, would encourage you and confirm your faith.

Isaiah 52 and 53 foretell Jesus's sacrifice through a fourth and final Servant Song with such clarity that skeptics can't explain the parallels except to say that Jesus must have intentionally modeled the details so people would know He was the Messiah.[8]

THE CALL TO LISTEN

READ ISAIAH 52:1-12. Describe in your own words what Isaiah said to God's people regarding:

• **Preparing to leave captivity (v. 1):**

• **His name (v. 6):**

• **The messenger He will send (v. 7):**

• **The manner in which they will leave (v. 12):**

This chapter began with more repeating words, "Awake, awake" (NASB, NIV), or "Wake up, wake up" (CSB, NLT)—these repetitions are another call to pay attention. Isaiah is waking us from the daydreaming of human effort and calling us to pay attention. Let's wake up today as we focus on the greatest message of all time—the truth that God sent His Son, Jesus, to die in our place so we could be made righteous through His sacrifice.

THE SERVANT'S SACRIFICE

After awakening his audience and predicting freedom from Babylonian captivity for God's people, Isaiah transitioned to the prophetic Servant's sacrifice that brings freedom for all people for all time.

READ ISAIAH 52:13–53:12. Using the chart, briefly describe the Servant according to each verse. Next, note any parallels to Jesus using the New Testament references I've given you in the last column.

ISAIAH PASSAGE	DESCRIPTION OF THE SERVANT	PARALLEL TO JESUS	NEW TESTAMENT REFERENCE
52:14-15	His face was disfigured so he hardly seemed human. He will startle many nations. Those who have never been told about him will see and understand.	Paul quoted these verses in Romans to describe Christ. The crown of thorns and beatings disfigured Jesus as Isaiah described.	Matthew 27:28-30; Romans 15:21
53:1			John 12:37-41; Romans 10:16-17
53:2-3			Matthew 27:22-25; John 1:46; John 12:37-43; John 15:20-21; John 19:1-3

ISAIAH PASSAGE	DESCRIPTION OF THE SERVANT	PARALLEL TO JESUS	NEW TESTAMENT REFERENCE
53:4-6			Matthew 8:14-17; 1 Peter 2:19-25
53:7-8			Luke 23:8-9,24-26; Acts 8:32-35
53:9			Matthew 27:57-60; Philippians 2:8; 1 Peter 2:19-25
53:12			Luke 22:36-38; Luke 23:34

What stood out most to you in these verses?

The description of Jesus as hardly recognizable as a human made me recall the depth of pain He endured. When I think that Jesus did this so the punishment for my sin could be transferred to Him, I feel the weight of it. I'm also captivated by the metaphor of sheep going astray. All people wander away from God's path like sheep. So God sent Jesus to be the "Lamb of God who takes away the sin of the world" (John 1:29). He gave Himself up for us as the perfect sacrifice to pay for our sins.

Though the original readers of Isaiah's words didn't have all the details, they learned that their righteousness would be found through a Servant sent on their behalf. Isaiah made it clear that ultimate victory over sin would come not through triumphant conquest but through an obedient Servant enduring rejection and abuse. It's important for us to understand Jesus willingly endured what we read about in Isaiah's prophecy.

Read the passages below and highlight any references to suffering, blood, or sacrifice.

When one of Jesus's disciples wanted to fight against the officers who came to make an arrest, Jesus said to him,

> Put your sword back into its sheath. Shall I not drink
> from the cup of suffering the Father has given me?
> JOHN 18:11

Earlier that night, Jesus hinted at what was to come for Him. During the last supper with His disciples, He foretold His substitutionary death:

> And he took a cup of wine and gave thanks to God for it. He gave it to
> them and said, "Each of you drink from it, for this is my blood, which
> confirms the covenant between God and his people. It is poured out as
> a sacrifice to forgive the sins of many. Mark my words—I will not drink
> wine again until the day I drink it new with you in my Father's Kingdom."
> MATTHEW 26:27-29

Jesus prepared His disciples as best He could. He also prayed for strength to endure the suffering He knew was coming while in the garden of Gethsemane. Colossians helps us feel the weight of what Christ's suffering accomplished for us:

> For God in all his fullness was pleased to live in Christ, and through him
> God reconciled everything to himself. He made peace with everything
> in heaven and on earth by means of Christ's blood on the cross.
> COLOSSIANS 1:19-20

How would you summarize in your own words what Christ's sacrificial death accomplished?

Our response to Isaiah 53 is to decide personally whether to accept or reject Jesus's sacrifice. Either write from memory or look up John 3:16 and write it here:

Each one of us must choose to believe and receive God's free gift. He said He would send a Messiah to save us, and He did.

Take a moment to reflect on your response to Christ's sacrifice on your behalf.
If you're a Christian, describe how and when you believed in God's love, sin's separation, and Christ's payment for sin to restore your relationship with God.

If you haven't accepted Christ's sacrifice personally, what is holding you back from making this decision today?

Every person will one day stand before God. The difference between eternal life with God or eternal separation from God will be what we believe about His Son. Passages like Isaiah 53 remind us that God went to great lengths to save us. It was a high price, but Jesus paid it for us.

As we reflect on the Servant in Isaiah 53, we find He didn't come just to tell us God's commands. He came in part to live in obedience to them for us. He came to exchange His life for ours. Righteousness comes not from doing our best but from putting our faith in Christ. Isaiah calls us to wake up to these truths.

Like sheep, we often leave God's paths to follow our own. We can't produce our own righteousness in our human strength. Only through trusting in Christ's sacrifice can we be made right with the holy God.

DAILY WRAP-UP

> **Today we focused on this truth: *Jesus bore the consequences for our disobedience.* How would you summarize your personal takeaway from today's study?**

PRAYER

Father, thank You that Your Son endured suffering and rejection on my behalf. I couldn't meet my greatest need, so You provided the way for my reconciliation to You. Awaken me often to these truths so I don't become numb to what You have done for me. You are my righteousness! Help me to strive less and trust You more. In Jesus's name, amen.

MEMORY VERSE ACTIVITY

Write down or say aloud Isaiah 50:10 from memory.

Session Five
GROUP TIME

REVIEW
Use the following Scripture passages and questions to discuss what you learned in your personal Bible study.

Recall the Big Ideas for each of the five days of study.

Share with the group how you filled in the blank on page 91.

Review your peace level as indicated on page 93. List ways Christians can stop trying so hard to find peace and instead trust God to give it.

Discuss your answers to the question, How is the Lord calling you away from striving on your own and toward relying on Him (p. 98)?

Talk about ways people might go through the motions spiritually and what helps us worship from the heart. (See pages 100-101.)

Read Isaiah 58:7-13. Share the practical ways you can live out God's commands in these verses. Refer to page 104 for guidance.

Look back at the chart on pages 109-110. Describe what stood out most to you in those verses.

MEMORIZE
Write Isaiah 50:10 on a poster or whiteboard in large print. Turn off the lights and use a flashlight to point to each word, reading it aloud as the light hits the word. Turn on the lights and recite the whole verse together.

WATCH

Use the fill-in-the-blanks and note-taking space as you watch the Session 5 teaching video together as a group.

Belief comes first and _____ flows out of that belief.

What's in your _____ will show up in your _____.

When there's a problem on the _____, we want to dig underneath to see what's going on _____.

_____ lie but _____ don't.

God asks us to _____ our hearts not _____ our behavior.

God's reaction to people's _____ is a call to _____.

How is your _____ life lately?
    One of the greatest ways you can listen to God is through _____ _____.

We need to _____ on dependency.

If we _____ God, we will _____ His commands.

WOW: _____

WOE: _____

NOTES

PRAY

Help us to trust that Your commands are good, Lord. Remind us when we struggle that Jesus isn't asking us to do something He didn't already do—He obeyed perfectly for us.

TRUST *God's* CORRECTION

SESSION SIX

Sometimes people get tripped up when they try to read through Isaiah and come to chapters 13–34. These passages include graphic descriptions of God's punishment of many nations. Reading them from our modern mindset can challenge our view of a loving and forgiving God. This week we'll explore these passages with a desire to know God and understand His righteous anger. His mercy will overshadow judgment, and we will see His discipline as a loving act—for us as well as for the original hearers of Isaiah's message. Together we'll discover how to get back on the right path when we've strayed. The seriousness of pride and arrogance in these chapters will help us embrace the humility plan. We'll see that Jesus is not only a Suffering Servant but also a righteous King who has the authority to correct us. While the Scriptures we read this week may surprise us at times, they are great reminders of the seriousness of sin and the mercy of our God.

BIG IDEA
We can trust the Lord's correction to help us get back on track when we turn toward sin.

Day One

HOPE AND JUDGMENT

As we read some passages this week that contain harsh language regarding God's judgment, we want to remember His intent. The Lord invites all people into relationship with Him, and one of His key character traits is justice. He is fair in all He does. We can trust that God will right the wrongs in our world in His way and in His time.

This week, we will focus our attention on what we can learn from examples of behaviors that consistently invited God's correction.

A GLIMPSE OF GOD'S CORRECTION

Since we can't comb through all of chapters 13–34 together, I'll quickly cover some of the highlights. You'll notice God's words of judgment for specific individuals, cities, and nations always followed sinful behaviors and patterns. The most common were pride, idol worship, oppression of others, self-sufficiency, and a lack of trust in God.

> Why would these behaviors need the Lord's correction? What do they say to God about a person's belief in and relationship with Him?

> List the opposite of each of these sins:
> - Pride:
>
> - Idolatry:
>
> - Oppression of others:
>
> - Self-sufficiency:
>
> - Lack of trust in God:

Why would behaviors and postures like the ones you just identified bring people into a closer relationship with God?

As you consider behaviors that brought correction and the opposite postures that brought relationship with God, can you identify any areas in your life where you can pursue the Lord more fully?

The Bible is clear: God offers a relationship with Himself to the entire world. He chose to use His people as His mouthpiece with His message, but He desired to be close with people of all nations—and that has always been the case. Sprinkled throughout these chapters of Isaiah are tender words about how the Lord longed for everyone to repent of sin and draw near to Him.

READ ISAIAH 19:18,21-25 in your Bible and underline verbs that describe what God would do in Egypt.

It's almost shocking for us to hear God refer to the nation of Egypt as "my people" (v. 25) considering their treatment of the Israelites, God's covenant people. But this is the perfect picture for us of the grace of the Lord. It's also important for us to understand God didn't bring painful consequences to the Egyptians or the Israelites for no reason. His intention was healing (v. 22), to help them get off the road that leads to destruction and onto the path of intimacy with Him. Pain helped them identify their need for God. He disciplined with the hope of turning them back in the right direction.

READ ISAIAH 27:7-8 in your Bible and underline God's reason for the exile.

Within these judgment chapters are sprinkled many verses regarding hope. God doesn't want to destroy His creation; He longs for them to be saved from damaging behaviors. Following the Lord means holding correction and judgment in one hand and hope in another. In faith, we hold both hands up in worship to God.

Obeying God isn't easy, but enduring His discipline doesn't seem enjoyable either. We get to pick our "tough." When we consider our choice to trust God or strive in human strength, I hope we choose trust time and again.

> **Think back on a time when you have felt the balance of God's correction and hope in your own life. What is one word you would choose to describe that experience or season?**

GOD'S HEART BEHIND HIS CORRECTION

READ ISAIAH 9:8–10:4. Then circle the words or phrases in the word bank below that angered the Lord. (Hint: There are eight to circle.)

PRIDE	HELPING THE NEEDY	TAKING ADVANTAGE OF ORPHANS	HYPOCRISY
ARROGANCE	WISE LEADERS	SPEAKING FOOLISHNESS	JUDGING FAIRLY
SEEKING GOD	FAILURE TO REPENT	INJUSTICE FOR THE POOR	WICKEDNESS

These verses highlight God's justice, one of His key attributes (or character traits). Let's admit that this language about the Lord's judgment is graphic and hard to read. I don't have any great explanations for those of you who are struggling with this strong language, but I know God is sovereign over everything, and He is serious about the right order of things.

The Hebrew word translated "justice" in Isaiah 10:2 is *mishpat*,[1] which "is much more than merely legality, as 'justice' has come to connote in English. Rather, it has the idea of 'right order.'"[2] God's justice always works together with His compassion and patience, as we see many times in the Old Testament (Ex. 34:6; Num. 14:18; Neh. 9:17; Ps. 86:15, etc.).[3]

Because God is just, He determines the right order for things in the world as well as in our lives:

- He sets the boundaries for morality (Ex. 20:1-17; Ps. 51:4).
- He disciplines justly (Heb. 12:5-11).
- His posture toward sin is wrath (Ex. 34:6-7; Rom. 6:23).
- He cares about the treatment of the poor and oppressed (Ps. 82:3; Luke 11:42; Jas. 1:27).

God is just—He knows how things should be ordered in your life. When you believe Him by faith, you are inspired to act justly. I pray today's conversation inspires you to get things in the right order as you consider the behaviors and attitudes that either separate people from God or draw them closer to Him. God doesn't delight in correction, but He also doesn't want you to stay on the wrong path. He will do what He must to draw you back to Him. Although His judgments can seem painful in the moment, you can trust that His goal leads to a hopeful place of intimacy with Him.

DAILY WRAP-UP

> Today we focused on this truth: *We can trust the Lord's correction to help us get back on track when we turn toward sin.* How would you summarize your personal takeaway from today's study?

PRAYER

Lord, I desire to follow You. Help me remain humble, dependent, and mindful of Your truths. When I begin to stray, help me to get back on the path of faith quickly. Sometimes Your justice is difficult to understand through my lens. Help me trust that You will ultimately make all things right. Please show me how I can be involved in helping the poor and oppressed! In Jesus's name, amen.

MEMORY VERSE ACTIVITY

Read Isaiah 38:16 aloud three times. You can find it printed on page 117.

Day Two
THE HUMILITY PLAN

God consistently corrected those who trusted in their own strength. As we try to strive less and trust God more, embracing humility will be a key posture for us. In order to trust, we must first admit our need for God.

BIG IDEA

Pride repeatedly brings God's correction into the lives of people and nations.

The tension we sometimes encounter in a discussion about pride is that we mistake godly confidence for pride. Taking initiative or boldly using our spiritual gifts shouldn't be equated with pride. Pride says, "I've got this!" Humility says, "God's got this!" Our ability to keep submitting to God's will over our own is what I sometimes refer to as the "humility plan." This plan realigns us to see our mistakes, failures, and problems as reminders of how much we need the Lord.

> **Where have you been on the humility plan lately? What has reminded you of your need for God?**

"If anyone would like to acquire humility, I can, I think, tell him the first step," said author C. S. Lewis. "The first step is to realize that one is proud. And a biggish step, too. At least, nothing whatever can be done before it. If you think you are not conceited, it means you are very conceited indeed."[4]

Today our goal is to see how our God responds to pride and seek His supernatural help to identify it.

BABYLON'S EXAMPLE

> **READ ISAIAH 13.** Describe Babylon's behavior that angered the Lord. (Pay close attention to v. 11.)

Babylon was a nation known for its pride, and God corrected their sinful behavior. Like yesterday's texts though, we'll find that judgment and hope remain intertwined.

READ ISAIAH 14:1-3. Circle the numbers that correspond to the blessings found in these verses for Israel. The Lord will:

1. Have mercy on them.
2. Make them rich with material possessions.
3. Choose them as His special people.
4. Bring them back to settle in their own land.
5. Give them easy lives with no challenges.
6. Bring people from many nations to help them return and serve them in the land.
7. Allow them to rule over their enemies.
8. Give them rest from sorrow, fear, slavery, and chains.

What comes next in Isaiah 14:4-23 is considered by scholars to be one of the finest Hebrew poems in all of Scripture. It includes four stanzas that are written in the form of a lament or funeral song. Let's briefly examine each of these stanzas and see what they teach us about the sin of pride and the Lord's correction.

1. The Earth's Reaction to the King's Death

READ ISAIAH 14:4-8. In your Bible, highlight phrases that reveal the earth's reaction to the death of this Babylonian king.

The earth could sing again; it was at rest because the king of Babylon could no longer destroy it. Pride is a destructive force that impacts not only people but the earth as well.

2. The Underworld's Response

READ ISAIAH 14:9-11. Describe briefly the scene taking place in the underworld.

The place of the dead was referred to in Hebrew as *Sheol*. These verses don't inform our theology of the afterlife but provide a poetic mockery of human pride. No matter how much you own, how much power you have, or how great you look, "each person is destined to die" (Heb. 9:27). As we move into the next stanza, notice a shift in language. Prophets often began with local events and then expanded to grander principles.

3. Heaven's Perspective

> **READ ISAIAH 14:12-15.** Identify three of several "I will" statements that mark this prideful figure.
>
> I will _____.
>
> I will _____.
>
> I will _____.
>
> Does it seem like these verses refer to a human king or to Satan? Jot down a few thoughts.

No matter what conclusions we draw, we can all agree that pride and godliness can't exist together. Those who desire to become God's equal by elevating themselves actually distance themselves from the living God. Jesus stepped down from glory and took on the role of a servant. He embodied humility to the point of death (Phil. 2:5-8). Our independence and self-sufficiency create a barrier between us and God. Humility draws us back to Him.

4. A Reflection of Life on Earth

> **READ ISAIAH 14:16-23.** Describe the burial of this king in a sentence.

This great king's body was left out in the streets or thrown into an unknown burial pit, which would have been an act of ultimate humiliation. For the original readers of Isaiah's poem, this king's dire end would connect his pride with severe judgment.

EXAMINING OUR OWN LIVES

As we reflect on Isaiah 13 and 14 and the pride of Babylon, we want to make connections to our own struggle with pride. These chapters shouldn't dissuade us from having ambition or pursuing big goals, but they remind us to regularly check our motives.

Compare and contrast what our culture says about what makes a person great and what God says.

CULTURE'S VALUES	GOD'S VALUES

What we learn from Isaiah 14 is that greatness is not found in striving to be more but in becoming less. This is the example Jesus set for us during His earthly ministry, and the way He teaches His followers to relate to others. For the Christian, the way up is down.

Ask the Lord to reveal any areas in your life where pride might be an issue. Then write your own "I will" statements themed with humility rather than pride.

I will _____.

I will _____.

I will _____.

You could have written a variety of phrases to fill in those blanks including release control, make prayer a priority, or choose to think of others more highly than myself. Isaiah's teaching regarding Babylon reminds us that pride leads to death but surrender leads to life. We can know beyond a shadow of a doubt that pride falls into that category for our heavenly Father. Because we know that pride brings consequences, we can embrace the humility plan.

DAILY WRAP-UP

Today we focused on this truth: *Pride repeatedly brings God's correction into the lives of people and nations.* How would you summarize your personal takeaway from today's study?

PRAYER

Lord, I want to humble myself before You. Pride comes naturally to me, but I know it doesn't honor You. Help me learn from Isaiah's message that pride leads to death, but surrendering to Your will leads to life. Correct me right away when I take steps toward striving on my own so that I can turn quickly toward trusting You more! In Jesus's name, amen.

MEMORY VERSE ACTIVITY

Read Isaiah 38:16 aloud one time. Then write it down in your book or on a separate piece of paper.

BIG IDEA
Repentance
is the goal of
God's correction.

Scholars have
suggested that Christ's
call for attention in
the parable of the
sower (Mark 4:3,9)
reveals the influence
of Isaiah 28:23-29,
which also used
farming metaphors
and called the
audience to listen.[6]

Day Three

TURN AROUND

Our God is a perfect parent. He doesn't have issues with being reactive or consistent. As we have already seen in Isaiah, God gives consequences to help people turn around when they are headed down the path of sin. This week's passages aren't the "feel good" Bible verses we find plastered on coffee cups or social media graphics. Reading about despair, destruction, and death brought by the Lord can be difficult to reconcile with the character of a loving and merciful God. But we know that "all Scripture is inspired by God" (2 Tim. 3:16), which means we need to lean into these chapters to see God's heart behind His correction.

GOD'S WAKE-UP CALL

Our God loves us too much to leave us on the path of destruction without sending up signal flares to get our attention, and nothing wakes us up from the trance of sin like pain. "Pain insists upon being attended to," said C. S. Lewis. "God whispers to us in our pleasures, speaks in our conscience, but shouts in our pains: it is his megaphone to rouse a deaf world."[5]

When something physically hurts in our bodies, it can mean an intervention is needed. A physician might need to set a bone, perform a surgery, or prescribe a medication. In the same way, our Great Physician may allow temporary discomfort in our lives for the greater good of long-term healing. God is willing to leverage our comfort to develop our character.

Let me be clear about one thing before you read any further: Not all pain in our lives comes from our own personal sin. Sometimes we are affected by others' sins or the general effects of living in a broken world. Some pain isn't our fault, but other times we bring it on ourselves. Either way, God doesn't waste our pain. He will use it to develop our character and strengthen our relationship with Him.

Through Isaiah's message, the Lord revealed His purposes for the nations' pain. Read the passages in the left column and fill in the missing information in the chart.

PASSAGE	PEOPLE	PAIN	PURPOSE
Isaiah 17:4-11	Israel	Desolate fields, few people remaining, grief	Verses 7-8
Isaiah 19:1-10,18-25	Egypt	Fighting, confused plans, cruel masters, Nile dried up, despair, workers will be sick at heart	Verse 22
Isaiah 20:1-6	Egypt and Ethiopia	Verse 3	Verses 5-6 So nations would look to the Lord instead of other nations for help
Isaiah 22:1-14	Jerusalem	Verses 2-5	Verses 9-13 So people would learn to mourn and show remorse for sin; to teach people to seek help from the Lord instead of trusting human strategies
Isaiah 27:7-13	Israel (again)	Houses abandoned, streets overgrown with weeds, broken people	Verses 8-9

What stood out to you as you read these verses about pain and God's purposes?

While the consequences of sin may have seemed harsh at times, we learn that God doesn't punish His children; He corrects them. His motive is not to abuse but to realign His creation. We see God's gentle methods spelled out with the analogy of a farmer in Isaiah 28.

What did the Lord identify as Samaria's downfall (Isa. 28:1,3,7-8)?

What did the priests and prophets say about God (28:9-10)?

What was the Lord's message to His people, and how did He communicate it (28:12-13)?

What do you think the Lord was trying to communicate about His correction with the illustration of the farmer (28:23-29)?

In agriculture, a farmer uses different procedures at different times. His work involves plowing, sowing, threshing and grinding with the goal of producing a harvest. Isaiah's illustration reminds us that God's purposes require Him to act according to the need of the season. He also doesn't refine every plant with the same method. Each crop is processed with the amount of pressure needed to produce the best end product. Like a farmer, the Lord will use the correct instrument to separate the worthless from the valuable in the harvest of our lives.

RESPONDING TO CORRECTION

Our pain can make us bitter against God or it can lead us to turn toward Him.

READ 2 CORINTHIANS 7:10 BELOW. Write your own definitions for *godly sorrow* and *worldly sorrow* in the spaces provided.

> For the kind of sorrow God wants us to experience leads us away from sin and results in salvation. There's no regret for that kind of sorrow. But worldly sorrow, which lacks repentance, results in spiritual death.
> 2 CORINTHIANS 7:10

- Godly sorrow:

- Worldly sorrow:

Godly sorrow turns us away from sin and toward God. *Worldly sorrow* refuses to turn away from sin. Both are reactions we may have when we experience the Lord's correction firsthand. When we understand God's correction is meant to help rather than harm, we can recognize God's discipline as an expression of love. God cares about us enough to discipline us (see Prov. 13:24). He does it so we might experience godly sorrow over sin and turn toward Him.

How have you grown closer to the Lord through a difficult season? Think back on specific painful circumstances and the lessons you learned.

What is one decision you can make or action you can take to turn away from sin and toward God today?

God longs for us to stop striving in our human strength and trust Him more. He wants us to look to our Creator for help when we go through seasons of discipline. When we get off the path of obedience to Him, He calls us out so that we can turn from sin and turn to Him. Today you may have sorrow, but know that it can be a godly sorrow that turns you in a hopeful direction.

DAILY WRAP-UP

Today we focused on this truth: *Repentance is the goal of God's correction.* How would you summarize your personal takeaway from today's study?

Day Four
REVIVAL

Spiritual sluggishness affects all of us from time to time, and the Lord longs to bring revival into our lives. In Isaiah 57:15 we find the word *revive,* which in Hebrew means to "enliven" or "to cause life."[7] Sin brings death, but the Lord longs to give us life.

God's correction can feel heavy as we've experienced this week in the pages of Isaiah. Today again we will find God's anger stirred up by disloyalty and depravity. But anger doesn't have the final word. God's mercy triumphs over judgment (Jas. 2:13). His goal is to bring revival to our spirits and minds so that we experience abundant life.

BIG IDEA
Sin brings death, but the Lord longs to give us life.

BARRIERS TO REVIVAL

Isaiah 57 is written as a Hebrew poem that confronts the nation of Israel's movement away from God and toward idolatry. The poem follows a format of mercy (vv. 1-2), judgment (vv. 3-13), and then once again mercy (vv. 14-21).

A witch or sorceress in Isaiah's day referred to "one who has opened herself to control by a spirit or supernatural entity."[8]

> **READ ISAIAH 57:1-2.** Explain how God shows mercy to those who follow godly paths.

Even though the righteous died and it seemed like no one cared, God cared and promised to give them peaceful rest. Despite death, His hope and mercy are still realized, and the wicked will not have the last word.

In the next section of Isaiah 57, we want to identify key behaviors that angered the Lord. These sins deadened their responsiveness to God.

READ ISAIAH 57:3-13. Answer the following multiple-choice questions:

1. What questions did the Lord have for the idol worshipers (v. 11)?

   A. Are you afraid of these idols?
   B. Is that why you lied to Me and forgot My words?
   C. Do you no longer fear Me because of My long silence?
   D. All of the above

2. What did the Lord say He would do regarding what the people saw as "good deeds" (v. 12)?

   A. Reward them
   B. Applaud them
   C. Expose them
   D. Forget them

3. Who did God say He would reward (v. 13)?

   A. Those who strive harder
   B. Those who worship idols
   C. Those who tolerate sin
   D. Those who trust in Him

God spoke through the prophet Isaiah to people who got way off track. God exposes sin so people can see the consequences of their choices. The people were determined and persistent but decidedly wrong. The objects of their affections were like smooth or slippery stones. Stones cannot speak, act, or move. They had "traded the truth about God for a lie" (Rom. 1:25). In the Lord's grace, He corrected them.

When we see the Israelites' behavior and God's strong reaction to it, we can exercise caution in our own lives. The apostle Paul wrote to his protégé Timothy about a people with parallel issues to those Isaiah described.

Answers: D, C, D

READ 2 TIMOTHY 4:3-4 BELOW. Underline the similarities between Isaiah 57:3-13 and these verses:

> For a time is coming when people will no longer listen to sound and wholesome teaching. They will follow their own desires and will look for teachers who will tell them whatever their itching ears want to hear. They will reject the truth and chase after myths.
> **2 TIMOTHY 4:3-4**

How do you see the need for this warning in our current culture?

We want to be alert and revived so that we are careful in these ways:

- We listen to sound and wholesome teaching;
- We don't follow our own desires;
- We don't look for teachers who will tell us only what we want to hear;
- We embrace the truth and reject myths.

Isaiah 57 reveals that God gets angry when we believe myths that appeal to our earthly lusts. The people combined following God with compromising His clear commands. They sought after any god or religion that they believed would reward them with material blessings and physical pleasure.

Today, the message of God's wrath toward sin is often downplayed in favor of emphasizing tolerance and self-expression. Itching ears would rather hear that we can practice behaviors that compromise God's truth *and at the same time* prop ourselves up with religious activities that make us feel spiritual. Isaiah's message assures us that we can't.

THE PATH TO REVIVAL

We can trust God's correction because He exposes sin to keep us from the consequences it brings. He also offers forgiveness and compassion to those who will turn from sin and turn to Him.

> **READ ISAIAH 57:14-21.** What did the Lord say to "clear away" (v. 14)? Who did the Lord say He would "restore" and "revive" (v. 15)?

> What did God promise to do—even for the greedy, stubborn people who made Him angry (vv. 18-19)?

> What outcomes are given for those who continue to reject the Lord (vv. 20-21)?

> Highlight or circle in your Bible all of the "I will" statements the Lord made in today's passage.

Earlier this week we read some "I will" prideful proclamations in Isaiah 14. Today, we find God telling us He will "heal," "lead," and "comfort" us (Isa. 57:18). Scripture tells us many times that our God is slow to anger and quick to compassion.

> **READ PSALM 103:8-14** in your Bible and circle any words or phrases that highlight God's grace and mercy.

In the original Hebrew of Isaiah 57:19 we find the word *shalom* twice. *Shalom* means, "completeness, soundness, welfare, peace."[9] God wants to give us the peace we so desperately desire, a peace that can only be found in Him. We won't find it in counterfeits or compromise. *Shalom* is at the heart of revival. The Lord longs to awaken us to more committed obedience to His ways because of His great love and compassion toward us.

I've been amazed over and over this week by the truth that the Lord loves me enough to correct me. He doesn't leave me on the path of sin without warnings and consequences to help me when I'm chasing the wrong things. Small compromises may not seem very serious in the moment, but today's chapter reminded me of the seriousness of sin. And as much as the Lord hates sin, He loves us so much more. I hope today you will hold on to the truth that He wants to heal you, lead you, and give you His peace!

Take some time to reflect on how you can be more fully committed to following God's path in your Christian walk. Write out a prayer asking the Lord to revive your heart.

DAILY WRAP-UP

Today we focused on this truth: *Sin brings death, but the Lord longs to give us life.* **How would you summarize your personal takeaway from today's study?**

PRAYER

Lord, revive me. Put new life in me that I might follow You more closely. Help me discern messages that lead me away from Your truth. Provide me with sound teaching rather than convenient messages that stroke my ego. Show me where I have compromised and lead me back to You. In Jesus's name, amen.

MEMORY VERSE ACTIVITY

Attempt to write out Isaiah 38:16 from memory, then check to see how you did.

BIG IDEA
Jesus will return and
bring perfect justice
to all creation.

Day Five

ALREADY, NOT YET

We aren't likely to trust the correction of someone we don't believe has the right to rule in our lives. I'm often skeptical of directives and authorities unless I believe they have a right to intervene in my life, or if I have willfully submitted myself to their leadership. I have no problem complying when I trust the rule-maker and rule-enforcer.

In our previous Day Five studies focused on the Messiah, we've seen Jesus depicted as our Suffering Servant. Today, we will see Him as a ruling authority. Jesus came to save, but when He returns a second time, it will be to rule. When we trust Him as our righteous Judge, we will be more open to His correction in our lives.

MESSIAH'S AUTHORITY

Isaiah employed the use of physical illustrations to reveal spiritual truths in Isaiah 11.

> **READ ISAIAH 11.** Draw or briefly describe one of the images or metaphors you find:

You had several illustrations to choose from in these verses—a shoot coming up out of a stump, a belt or sash, predators and prey, or a highway. Let's look at each of these individually and see how they reveal Jesus as the Messiah with authority to rule in the lives of all creation.

1. A shoot from the stump of David (vv. 1-2)

The stump with a "new Branch" (11:1) represents the Messiah, Jesus, coming from the line of David, and the Spirit of the Lord would "rest on him" (v. 2).

> List some of the words used in Isaiah 11:2-4 to describe the Messiah's rule.

Isaiah identified the stump with Jesse, who was King David's father. This reference to Jesse connects the Messiah with the line of David.

> How do these qualities deepen your trust in Jesus's authority to direct and correct in your life?

The Lord will never get it wrong, so we can trust His correction. He doesn't judge according to outward appearances or gossip. He has all the evidence, knows every motive, and is able to judge fairly.

2. A belt and sash (vv. 3-5)

The next metaphor we discover in Isaiah 11 is a belt and sash. Isaiah 11:5 says of the Messiah, "Righteousness will be his belt and faithfulness the sash around his waist" (NIV). A Hebrew sash was less like a waist ribbon and more like an "undergarment" (NLT). This "belt or sash (v. 5) was the garment that gave stability to the whole ensemble."[10] This image reveals that Christ was fully prepared for judgment with righteousness and truth as His foundation. His reign is held together by truth inside and out.

3. Predators and prey (vv. 6-9)

When Jesus returns in the future, He will fully restore peace to the earth. At that time, hostility between predators and prey will no longer exist. As we read this glimpse into the reign of the Messiah as King, we must acknowledge that although Jesus partially fulfilled these prophetic metaphors when He came to earth the first time, they have not fully come to pass on earth yet. The oppressed still seek justice, babies can't play near cobra's nests, and lions and lambs aren't lying down together.

We can't say exactly how these prophecies have been or will be fulfilled, but we can best understand them with the words *already* and *not yet*. Jesus has *already* fulfilled Isaiah 11 in that He came to earth as the righteous Branch. But elements of these verses have not yet been fulfilled.

It makes me think about the glimpse we get of Jesus's eternal reign in Revelation 20–21. During the future reign of Christ, the earth will be free of aggression and chaos. This seems to be precisely what Isaiah described. Jesus has already come, but He will come again. The next time it will not be as the Servant in the songs we've studied in Isaiah. His next appearance will be characterized as a reigning King who restores all of creation.

4. The higher path (v. 16)

Isaiah closed this chapter with the image of a highway, one of Isaiah's favorite images.[11] The highway Isaiah had in mind isn't a literal road; it's a spiritual journey. Jesus is the Messiah who bridges the gap that sin created between the Father and His creation. Jesus's saving work has three key elements. In each one, we can clearly see the *already* and *not yet* at work in our individual relationships with Jesus.

- **Justification:** We become saved from the penalty of sin the moment we believe in our heart and confess with our mouth that Jesus is Lord (Rom. 10:9).

- **Sanctification:** We are being saved from the power of sin as God conforms us more and more to the image of His Son. This is an ongoing process that lasts our whole lives (Rom. 6–8).

- **Glorification:** We will be saved from the presence of sin when we are in heaven after our physical death or the return of Christ (1 Cor. 15).

Our salvation has happened, is happening, and will happen more fully when we trade this body for a new one! This leads us to praise the One who makes all this possible (2 Cor. 5).

Some references to roads, paths, and highways in Isaiah:

- Isaiah 26:7-8
- Isaiah 35:8
- Isaiah 40:3-4
- Isaiah 42:16
- Isaiah 49:11
- Isaiah 57:14
- Isaiah 62:10

READ ISAIAH 12 slowly as a prayer of praise to the Lord. Then write out the verse that most resonates with you.

We don't need to question our Messiah's authority. We can trust His correction because His will is to save us. I pray you will worship Him for what He has already done and live with expectant hope for the *not yet* that is still to come.

DAILY WRAP-UP

Today we focused on this truth: *Jesus will return and bring perfect justice to all creation.* How would you summarize your personal takeaway from today's study?

MEMORY VERSE ACTIVITY

Write down or say aloud Isaiah 38:16 from memory.

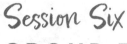

Session Six
GROUP TIME

REVIEW

Use the following Scripture passages and questions to discuss what you learned in your personal Bible study.

Recall the Big Idea for each of the five days of study.

Read Isaiah 9:8–10:4. Discuss what is difficult for you to accept from this passage and why.

Share your three "I will" statements from page 124.

Read 2 Corinthians 7:10 on page 129 and discuss your definitions for godly sorrow and worldly sorrow. Describe how godly sorrow is helpful.

Read 2 Timothy 4:3-4 on page 133 and share your answer to the question, How do you see the need for this warning in our current culture?

Review Isaiah 11:2-4. Talk about the words you listed to describe the Messiah's rule on page 137 and how they encourage you today.

MEMORIZE

Give each girl a piece of cardstock and various colored markers, colored pencils, pens, or crayons. Tell them to create word art, or simply write out Isaiah 38:16. Invite each girl to present her word art and read the verse aloud. When she reads aloud, encourage other group members to say the verse along with her.

WATCH

Use the fill-in-the-blanks and note-taking space as you watch the Session 6 teaching video together as a group.

We need to trust God's _____.

We're either going to view the world through the lens of
_____ or we're going to view _____
through the lens of the world.

_____ tells the truth.

Two sins God corrected:
　　1. _____ (Isa. 26:4-6)

　　2. _____ and _____ of the poor

We don't want to exchange the plans of a good _____ for the schemes of an evil _____.

God's pressure points are _____ (Isa. 28:23-29).

There's no one wiser than _____.

WOW: _____

WOE: _____

NOTES

PRAY

God, You are a good and loving Father. Thank You for loving us enough to correct us. Help us to welcome Your warnings and follow as You correct our course.

TRUST *God's* COMING

SESSION SEVEN

can't believe we've come to the last week in our study of Isaiah! This week we'll get some glimpses into Christ's return to motivate us toward holy living now. The prophet reminds us that while the world often feels chaotic, the best is yet to come. He'll show us some practical postures—like prayer and praise—we can take as we wait for the future perfection Jesus will bring. Isaiah will also help us assess next steps to take when we feel stuck in our doubts and questions, and he'll help us learn to live with eternity in view. But he won't paint everything as rosy. We close out our study with a reminder that judgment awaits those who don't believe in Jesus. I pray this will motivate us to cling to the gospel and not let anyone we love slip into eternity unwarned or unprayed for.

MEMORY VERSE

For since the world began, no ear has heard and no eye has seen a God like you, who works for those who wait for him!

ISAIAH 64:4

BIG IDEA

We can trust that
Jesus will return and
put an end to our
earthly suffering.

Day One

THE BEST IS YET TO COME

Whether you have a trip, graduation, milestone birthday, or new season of life on the horizon, thinking about fun in the future can help us through dreary days.

> **Think about something you are looking forward to in the next year. Do you feel good about the level of details you know? Why or why not?**

As we focus on the return of Christ in our study this week, we will find that we can get excited about the details revealed in prophecy and embrace the mystery of future surprises. We can trust God for a hopeful future, believing Jesus will return and put an end to our suffering.

LIGHT IN THE DARKNESS

I know Jesus is going to come back, but it can be tough to keep that perspective at the front of my mind. Disappointments and difficulties regularly threaten my positive outlook, so I love how Isaiah began this last section of his book with a call to remember the bright future the Lord has in store for His followers.

> **READ ISAIAH 60:1-3.** List some repeated words from these verses.

In the last seven chapters of Isaiah, we find the word *glory* many times. Because you have the promise that God's light and glory will last forever, you can rise and shine above this present and temporary darkness.

> **The glory of the Lord can be a tough concept to grasp. How would you define "the glory of the Lord" in your own words?**

Unger's Bible Dictionary defines God's glory as "the manifestation of His divine attributes and perfections, or such visible splendor as indicates the possession and presence of these . . . God's glory is that in which holiness comes to expression."[1] We began our study of Isaiah with a focus on trusting God's character. Holiness was highlighted in Isaiah's vision of God on His throne (Isa. 6). And we found God's name as the *Holy One of Israel* throughout the pages of Isaiah's book. Glory is the expression of God's holiness.

Pastor Warren Wiersbe said, "When God's glory is on the scene, everything becomes new."[2] What challenges in your life make all things becoming new sound good to you right now?

We've all faced moments in life that left us wondering, *Where is God in this?* Through the prophet Isaiah, God gives us a vision of restoration— a time when all creation will return to its perfect, original state.

In Isaiah 60:4-18 we find prophecies of hope regarding the future. Which one stands out most to you?

READ ISAIAH 60:20-22. Describe in your own words what will happen in the future.

The emphasis on light in the opening verses of Isaiah 60 provides a contrast to the preceding chapter, which stressed the darkness: "We look for light but find only darkness. We look for bright skies but walk in gloom" (Isa. 59:9b).[3]

Scholars often connect Isaiah 60 with John 17 in the New Testament where the theme of "glory" appears repeatedly in Jesus's prayer that the Father would glorify Him so He could glorify the Father.[4]

The Lord will provide light without the sun and moon one day. Revelation gives us more details about this future time:

> And the city has no need of sun or moon, for the glory of God illuminates the city, and the Lamb is its light.
> **REVELATION 21:23**

What from Isaiah 60 makes you most excited about the future?

God's mercy, peace, righteousness, and everlasting light eradicating injustice, difficulty, and darkness sounds incredible to me. Future glory on display reminds us that the best is yet to come—for our lives, yes, but also for the entire world. Isaiah continued into the next chapter with a hopeful message, particularly for those experiencing oppression.

HOPE FOR THE HOPELESS

Some older commentators have debated whether Isaiah 61 contains a fifth Servant Song because it refers to the Messiah, but most modern scholars do not share this view, saying only four Servant Songs are found in Isaiah 42; 49; 50; and 52–53.[5]

READ ISAIAH 61:1-3. Circle the letter that best answers the question: Who are identified as the recipients of good news, comfort, and freedom?

A. The poor

B. The brokenhearted

C. The captives/prisoners

D. Those who mourn

E. All of the above

What good things can be anticipated?

The Lord also revealed that He would plant His people like great oak trees of right living (v. 3). These verses reassure us that while we suffer and need comfort now, in the future we can anticipate the ashes of our struggles to be transformed into crowns of beauty. We can trust that every struggle we experience has an expiration date. Thanks to the Gospel of Luke, we know Jesus is the One these verses reference.

READ LUKE 4:16-21 in your Bible and underline Jesus's words after His public reading of Isaiah 61.

Jesus shared the good news that He was the anticipated Messiah. He didn't beat around the bush when it came to His identity as the restorer of all creation. With His first coming He sacrificed His life as the final payment for sin. Jesus rose again in victory with the promise to return. When He comes again, we will see an even greater fulfillment of Isaiah 61.

READ ISAIAH 61:4-11. List the illustrations Isaiah used to communicate the joy that is coming (vv. 10-11).

Isaiah's descriptions of eternity include pictures of new clothes, a bride and groom dressed and adorned with jewels for their wedding, and a garden in early spring with plants sprouting everywhere. While you might not have thought about planning a wedding or planting a garden, you've probably planned a party for a friend or written a paper. And most people don't do that haphazardly. The organization is deliberate, so that when the time is right all the details come together to produce something amazing. Only God the Father knows when Jesus will return (Mark 13:32), but His coming has been prearranged. In the meantime, we can trust that Jesus is coming back. And when He does, we will experience His glory and light rather than the suffering and discouragement we often encounter here on earth. Truly, the best is yet to come!

DAILY WRAP-UP

Today we focused on this truth: *We can trust that Jesus will return and put an end to our earthly suffering.* How would you summarize your personal takeaway from today's study?

PRAYER

Lord, I'm so glad You have a plan—a good plan. Help me not to give into despair based on the bad news all around me. I want to live with joyful anticipation of the future You have in store. Thank You for being a God who brings beauty from ashes, restores what's been lost, and brings glory and light into my life. In Jesus's name, amen.

MEMORY VERSE ACTIVITY

Read Isaiah 64:4 aloud three times. You can find it printed on page 143.

BIG IDEA
While we wait, we
can pray and praise.

Day Two

IN THE MEANTIME

Waiting is one of my least favorite things. Recently, a deer hit my minivan and caused a lot of damage—both to the deer and my car. As an excessive planner, waiting to hear back from the body shop was painful for me. I kept looking at used cars and obsessively wondering how I would drive to all the places I needed to go that week—all less than twenty-four hours after my wreck! I knew I needed to wait patiently and just see how things would unfold, but I wanted something productive to *do* in the meantime.

**What is something you are waiting for right now?
How are you handling the waiting?**

Restlessness and impatience often come when we feel uncertain about the future—even something small. But if we can learn to trust God in the little things, we strengthen our trust muscle with the bigger things in life.

Throughout Isaiah we've seen that a relationship with Jesus is more about *being* in His presence than *doing* certain things. This aligns with our focus on striving less and trusting God more. However, today we will discover that there are some things we can do in our waiting that will strengthen our trust in God and temper our tendencies toward excessive planning. Isaiah 62 and 63 reveal that right responses to the reality of Jesus's second coming include prayer and praise.

PRAY FOR THE FUTURE

READ ISAIAH 62:1-12 and describe what Isaiah's prayers in verse 1 and the watchmen's prayers in verses 6-7 have in common.

Isaiah said he would not stop praying and posted watchmen to pray day and night. Most Christians would agree that prayer is important, yet many of us struggle with a disconnect in what we believe and how we act when it comes to prayer. People often view prayer as something to do when you desperately want God to do something you desire. But prayer exists to align us to God's will, not to inform Him of ours. Isaiah focused more on God's promises than his own agenda in prayer.

What are some things you have been asking God for lately?

Now consider those same requests framed in this sentence: Lord, Your will be done with _____.

Prayer allows us to release control and trust God with our present situations as well as our future worries. Sometimes it feels like things aren't moving as fast as we think they should. With things like texts and snaps and two-day shipping, we've been conditioned to expect quick responses. When this expectation for instant gratification seeps into our prayer lives, it creates some fundamental problems.

But Isaiah teaches us to pray like watchmen.[6] Watchmen spent many hours waiting and watching. Isaiah said those who give the Lord no rest until He completes His work are like watchmen who are looking out in all directions and praying for God to do what He promised. Watchmen (or watchwomen) pray with expectation but leave the timing in the Lord's hands. And Jesus taught the same thing.

READ LUKE 11:5-10. Summarize what you learn about prayer from the story Jesus told.

Watchmen would sit up in towers so they could see in every direction.[7] The Hebrew word for *watchman* comes from the word *shamar*, which means "to keep, guard, observe, give heed, to watch for, to wait for."[8]

These instructions from Isaiah and Jesus do not mean begging God will twist His arm into action. But they do challenge us to pray consistently and intentionally. As we pray more, our trust in God is strengthened, which creates a healthy cycle that looks like this:

TRUST   **PRAYER**

In the pages of Isaiah, we can see ourselves as watchmen (or watchwomen) who wait and pray with shameless persistence realizing the connection, alignment, trust, and change that can occur through regular communication with God.

PRAISE GOD TODAY

READ ISAIAH 63:7-14. Then fill in the blanks with the three things Isaiah said he would do in verse 7.

> I will tell of the LORD's unfailing love. I will praise the LORD
> for all he has done. I will rejoice in his great goodness to
> Israel, which he has granted according to his mercy and love.
> **ISAIAH 63:7**

• I will _____.

• I will _____.

• I will _____.

Isaiah worshiped the Lord while he waited. Worship is about assigning worth and adoration to the Lord, and we can do this in a variety of ways.

What are some ways you worship the Lord?

We can worship God in many ways, including through singing, giving, serving, praying, journaling, silently praising God in our minds, speaking words of praise out loud, and obeying God's commands, just to name a few. Isaiah wrote words of praise to God as the

Savior (63:8), Redeemer (63:9), Spirit who "gave them rest" (63:14), and Leader with "a magnificent reputation" (63:14). Praise is an element of prayer that helps us remember God's greatness. Without it, we can begin to see ourselves with big problems and a small God. Worship realigns us to the bigness of our God, which puts our struggles into perspective.

Take three minutes to align your behavior with your belief, using one of the choices below:

☐ **Listen to a worship song.**
☐ **Write words of praise in your journal.**
☐ **Make a list of God's attributes.**
☐ **Use the alphabet to identify words that describe God.**
☐ **Other:** _____.

Isaiah's prayer and praise hit close to home for me. Impatience is a problem this watchwoman is always on the lookout for. I love that Isaiah shows us some things we can do while we wait, despite any circumstances we face. These verses also give us needed perspective as we wait for Jesus to return.

DAILY WRAP-UP

Today we focused on this truth: *While we wait, we can pray and praise.* **How would you summarize your personal takeaway from today's study?**

BIG IDEA
God's silence
doesn't indicate
His absence.

Day Three

ARE WE THERE YET?

Every time he got in my car this twelve-year-old boy was full of questions. We were doing respite care for another foster family while they were on vacation, and no matter how long the drive, he wanted to know every detail. This happened so many times that I finally assured him he could trust me. He didn't have to know because wherever he went with me—he would be safe. I asked him to trust me with the specifics. All he needed to do was sit back, relax, and enjoy the ride.

While I can coach someone else on trusting during a trip, I can't always practice what I preach. I know Jesus is coming back, but I have a lot of questions about when, where, and how He will return, not to mention why it's taking so long! Maybe you question whether Jesus will return during your lifetime. Or you may wonder how the events of the end times will unfold and how much we should be prepared for these things. We all have questions because of the contrast between what we know about God from His Word and our experiences in everyday life.

When the Lord isn't handling things the way we think He should, it can be frustrating. Isaiah sets a great example for us in today's texts, because he wasn't shy about bringing his questions to God. He worked through his doubts and questions with the Lord to move from a place of frustration to trust.

When we feel stuck because God doesn't seem to be doing what we think He should, Isaiah reminds us that our conversations with the Lord can be raw and real. In fact, they need to be for us to wrestle through the contradictions we encounter as we seek to trust God in a broken world. In Isaiah 63–64, we will discover that Isaiah followed this pattern we can model: (1) complain to the Creator; (2) ask for action; and (3) recognize roles.

COMPLAIN TO THE CREATOR

READ ISAIAH 63:15-19. Write out one of Isaiah's complaints in your own words.

Isaiah asked God to look down from heaven and see. He complained about God's absence in the lives of His people and said, "Sometimes it seems as though we never belonged to you, as though we had never been known as your people" (Isa. 63:19). In some seasons Isaiah felt God's presence strongly—like his vision of heaven in Isaiah 6. But here we find Isaiah in a low moment, complaining about God's silence and asking questions about His lack of intervention. He acknowledged the Lord as "Father" and "Redeemer from ages past" (v. 16), while at the same time admitting enemies had destroyed the "holy place" (v. 18).

We don't know who else Isaiah shared his frustrations with, but I love it that he brought them to the Lord. I find that when I bring my complaints first to my Creator and work through them in my journal or on my knees in prayer, I am then able to share my feelings with family and friends from a healthier perspective.

What current frustrations do you need to bring before the Lord, rather than taking them somewhere else? Journal a few sentences telling the Lord how you feel about His action or inaction, whether in your life personally or in the world at large.

References to God as Father are prevalent in the New Testament but very rare in the Old Testament. This is why it's amazing that we find two references to God as Father in Isaiah 63:16 and will encounter another mention of Father in 64:8.

We can press into our doubts and questions instead of running from them. Being human means having emotions—and this means sometimes we feel like God doesn't see us or won't act to help us. After Isaiah's complaints, he then asked God to act.

ASK FOR ACTION

READ ISAIAH 64:1-4. Describe in your own words what Isaiah asked the Lord to do in verse 1.

Most scholars believe Isaiah was referring to the exodus in his request for God to burst down from heaven. The Lord shook a mountain (Ex. 19:16-19) and revealed Himself to His people.[9]

Isaiah asked the Lord to "burst from the heavens and come down" (v. 1). He wanted to see God act in glory and power like He had in the past. Isaiah knew he didn't serve a fake god like those of the surrounding nations. His God is real. The Holy One of Israel parted the Red Sea (Ex. 14:21), held back the rain for forty days (1 Kings 17:1), and made city walls fall to the ground (Josh. 6:20). So, Isaiah asked God to do it again—to act in his own day—to burst down from heaven and intervene.

When we are confused by our circumstances, we can petition God to intervene because He is real. We have seen Him work in our hearts before, and we know He can do it again. He invites us to ask Him for help and trust Him to do what He says He will do in His Word.

The apostle Paul quoted part of Isaiah 64:4 (our memory verse this week) to remind the church that God still acts on behalf of those who wait for Him (1 Cor. 2:9).

Jot down a few sentences asking God to act in your heart, mind, or circumstances.

Even though Isaiah felt at one point like his people had never belonged to God, he asked God to come and show Himself real again. He acknowledged his doubts but leaned into his faith. These postures of complaining (to our Creator) and asking (for God to act) can help us move spiritually toward greater trust in God. When God seems silent in our lives, remember He is never absent. When He feels far away, ask Him to reveal Himself to you again.

RECOGNIZE ROLES

> **READ ISAIAH 64:5-12.** Summarize the roles of God and humans below. (Hint: There are no "right" answers, so use your own words to describe Isaiah's insights.)
>
> People are characterized by _____ (vv. 5-7).
>
> God is _____ (v. 8).

I hope you noticed the three references to sin associated with people in these verses. They may strive to do good, but their deeds are like filthy rags (Isa. 64:6). The Lord is our Father who provides, protects, and disciplines us. He is also the Potter, the One in control to mold and shape us into His design.

As the clay, we are prone to sin and don't always have a clear picture of the master plan. This is why it is so important that we remember God is our Potter, and we can trust Him to mold us and guide us in the way we need to be. Understanding this relationship allows us to trust God's promises. He will burst down from heaven at just the right time. I may think it should be today, but He knows best.

Knowing Isaiah felt the freedom to bring his complaints and questions to God reminds us that we can be brutally honest in our prayers and bold in our petitions. God's sovereign hand is at work in our lives and our world, even when we don't feel it.

DAILY WRAP-UP

Today we focused on this truth: *God's silence doesn't indicate His absence.* How would you summarize your personal takeaway from today's study?

PRAYER

Lord, I struggle to understand everything happening around me. Help me to remember that I can bring my complaints directly to You. Forgive me for sometimes complaining to everyone around me but You. I'm asking You to act—come and burst down from heaven and return. Thank You for the reminder that even though I think You should come back today, You are Sovereign in Your timing and plan! In Jesus's name, amen.

MEMORY VERSE ACTIVITY

Write down Isaiah 64:4. Also record one thought you have as you read over this verse.

BIG IDEA
God promises
us more than
just this life.

Day Four

ANOTHER TIME, ANOTHER PLACE

Today I had a conversation with myself after my alarm went off. If I stayed in bed and skipped my morning exercise class, then I could sleep an extra hour and my muscles (sore from yesterday's class) could get a break. Would rest or movement be the right choice for today? I asked my current self what my future self would say was best. With a groan, I threw back the covers and headed to the gym. My future self was right; it felt good to stretch, move, and connect with my workout buddies first thing.

What's a choice (big or small) that you've made recently where you considered possible consequences in making your decision?

We often evaluate the future impact as part of our decision-making process. This is important to do in our walk with God, too. Thankfully, the Bible provides us with important details about the future so that we can make holy choices as we prepare for Christ's return. This week our focus has been on trusting God's promises about Jesus's return, but that day often feels so far into the future that it doesn't affect my current decisions. Prophetic passages—like the one we will cover in Isaiah today—can feel disconnected from our day-to-day lives. But through God's revealed glimpses of the future, we can live with the end in mind.

In the final pages of his vision, Isaiah wrote about the future. In Isaiah 65, God answered the lament written by Isaiah on behalf of the people of Israel (Isa. 63–64) with a word of hope for their future—the joy of eternity in His presence.

OUR CURRENT STATE

READ ISAIAH 65:1-16. What are a few of the ways the Lord said the people of Israel had provoked Him (vv. 3-7)?

List a few of the blessings the Lord described for His servants, the remnant of His people who would seek Him (vv. 8-16).

In Isaiah 65, God spoke to the nation's blind spots. He allowed their doubts and questions but wanted them to understand how they contributed to His judgment. The Israelites asked why God wasn't intervening in their circumstances to ease their suffering. The Lord explained how they had provoked Him to anger. However, God also acknowledged that not everyone had resorted to human striving.

The Lord illustrated this principle with a description of grapes that shouldn't be destroyed because they still had some good in them. This good wasn't characterized by superior life performance or religious rituals but an attitude of seeking God (Isa. 65:8-10). After addressing the people's lament, the Lord revealed spiritual realities that will take place in the future.

"'The Valley of Achor' was the place where Achan was stoned to death because he disobeyed the Lord (Josh. 7). When the Lord restores His estranged wife, Israel, the Valley of Achor will become for them 'a door of hope' (Hos. 2:15)."[10]

OUR FUTURE REALITY

READ ISAIAH 65:17-25. Draw lines to identify whether each one is a current or future event.

- A new heaven and new earth exist.
- Former things won't be remembered.
- The sound of weeping and crying.
- A baby dies after only a few days of life.
- An old man who dies at one hundred will be considered a youth.
- The wolf and lamb will feed together.

CURRENT

FUTURE

Isaiah reminded his readers that another time is coming in the future that won't be like our time. Most scholars identify this period as the eternal kingdom of Christ (Rev. 21) because in the eternal state, people will not get old and die (Isa. 65:20).[11] We can't know for certain the timeline of these future events or the details of how God will bring about

His eternal plan, but we can focus on how our behaviors today will affect our future.[12] God has a sovereign plan that will be accomplished, but our decisions matter. As we navigate our days in the meantime, we can seek the Lord and trust Him more, or we can rely on counterfeits and provoke Him with disobedience.

How does Isaiah's glimpse into the future encourage you spiritually?

"Oh, that we might know the LORD! Let us press on to know him. He will respond to us as surely as the arrival of dawn or the coming of rains in early spring" (Hos. 6:3).

Isaiah's descriptions of a future time remind me that this life is not all there is. It helps me view my blessings and challenges with greater perspective. When I get caught up in the temporary stuff of this life, an eternal lens helps me refocus on what will matter most in the next. Concerns over everything from busy schedules, college applications, team tryouts, or friend drama won't overwhelm us as much when we consider them in light of eternity. We can't ignore them, but they don't have to rock our world.

EMBRACING THE IN BETWEEN

Many passages in the New Testament give us further clarity on how we should live in light of Christ's second coming.

READ TITUS 2:11-13 in your Bible, and note words or phrases that instruct us how to live as we trust the promise of Jesus's return.

In light of God's salvation, we are to live lives of repentance, turning from sin and toward the Lord. This is an ongoing posture we take as we desire to seek the Lord and draw near to His heart. God wants His people close, so He reveals Himself and provides clarity about what pleases Him and what doesn't.

Think about your life. Ask the Lord to reveal any ways you can increase your devotion to Him. (Remember that this is not about working harder but learning to trust Him more.) Record any thoughts that come to mind below.

I need constant reminders of God's good plan for the future because I so easily drift into obsessing over the stuff of this life. I get stuck in the day and need to be awakened to a greater vision of what God is doing. Thinking about God's plan for the future reminds me that my decisions matter. When we stand before the Lord at the end of our earthly lives, things like scrolling social media, joining another club or sport, or attending every Friday night football game will not seem like proper excuses for failing to seek Him. The Lord offers us the opportunity today to get to know Him more through His Word, through prayer, and through His body, the church. I hope the thought of a future with peace, no tears, and Christ ruling the earth brings a smile to your face and conviction to your heart as you seek to live a life today that honors God.

DAILY WRAP-UP

Today we focused on this truth: *God promises us more than just this life.* How would you summarize your personal takeaway from today's study?

PRAYER

Lord, help me remember that I'm not aimlessly wandering through my life. You have a plan. I can hardly wrap my mind around the future when Christ will return to rule on earth. Help me live in the light of that day—to make decisions that honor You today. Thank You for revealing Your plan to give me hope and strength as I wait for Your perfect timing. In Jesus's name, amen.

MEMORY VERSE ACTIVITY

Attempt to write out Isaiah 64:4 from memory, then check to see how you did.

BIG IDEA
Jesus makes the
difference between
eternal life and
eternal separation
from God.

Prophecy helps us:

- **Answer questions we have about eternity;**

- **Keep perspective in our current trials;**

- **Pursue a life of obedience in light of the future benefits of holy living;**

- **Deepen our faith in God's trustworthiness;**

- **Recognize God's relentless love and forgiveness for His creation.**

Day Five

HAPPILY EVER AFTER

If I'm going to invest my time in a movie's characters and story, then I want it all to work out in the end. Something in us loves happily ever afters, maybe because they rarely unfold in our real lives like they do in the movies. While the end of Isaiah won't leave us with a feel-good resolution, it will remind us of the very important reality of God's judgment and hope.

Before we dive into the last chapter of Isaiah, I want to highlight why studying Old Testament prophecy matters.

READ 2 PETER 1:19b-21. What did Peter our attitude toward prophecy should be?

We navigated the deep waters of Isaiah—just like Peter instructed! Peter said the words of prophets are light in a dark place, a metaphor Isaiah used often to encourage trust in the Lord. Many of his prophecies point to Jesus, who is "the light of the world" (John 8:12). Today, we will not find specific Messianic references, but we will highlight this important gospel truth: Jesus makes the difference between eternal life and eternal separation from God.

STRIVING LESS

READ ISAIAH 66:1-6. Identify the qualities that please and displease the Lord:

Who will God bless (v. 2)?

Who will God reject (vv. 3-4)?

Throughout the book of Isaiah, we've identified serious problems like ritualism (focus on religious rituals instead of God), hypocrisy, and pride. People came up with their own way to relate to God. The Lord called to them, but they turned a deaf ear to His instructions in favor of their own plans. They strived more and trusted less.

We face the same challenge. Even after we have committed our lives to Christ, confessing our sin and need for a Savior, we struggle to keep depending on the Lord. God is clear in His words through Isaiah: "I will bless those who have humble and contrite hearts, who tremble at my word" (v. 2). The Lord is to have the first place in my life.

What have you discovered about striving less and trusting God more over the course of our study in the book of Isaiah?

TRUSTING MORE

READ ISAIAH 66:7-24. What did the Lord promise Jerusalem (vv. 12-13)?

How will the Lord punish the world (vv. 15-16)?

What did Isaiah say will happen in the future (v. 23)?

Now, if I were Isaiah, I would have ended the book at verse 23 with a hopeful word for the future, the happily ever after when everyone will worship the Lord. But Isaiah left a final warning for those who rebel against God:

REREAD ISAIAH 66:24. Summarize the warning Isaiah gave.

The images in this verse shock us and leave us with a sobering reminder of the eternal plight of those who do not confess with their mouths and believe in their hearts that Jesus is Lord (Rom. 10:9). This reality should motivate us to evaluate our own salvation and share the gospel with those we know who are far from God.

We all have a choice: we can humbly seek God in faith and trust His plan over ours, or we can strive to live in our own strength and follow our own plan. We often talk about the positive benefits of being a Christian but sometimes fail to warn people of the risk of refusing God's invitation. Charles Spurgeon said, "If hell must be filled, let it be filled in the teeth of our exertions, and let not one go unwarned and unprayed for."[13]

> Journal a short prayer on an index card thanking God that your eternity is secure because of Jesus. Keep this card with you as a comforting reminder that your salvation is secure in Jesus.

> Name someone far from God whom you don't want to slip into eternity unprayed for. Pray for them now.

Verse 24 is not all bad news. If you're in Christ, then Isaiah's final warning is a reminder that God will make good on His promise to eliminate sin and all its effects once and for all. You can anticipate the end of your life with joy knowing Jesus is the Messiah foretold in the book of Isaiah, and He will keep His promise to return. The New Testament spells it out clearly:

> Whoever has the Son has life; whoever does
> not have God's Son does not have life.
> 1 JOHN 5:12

We can't keep Jesus's saving power to ourselves. If we love people, then we will share with them not only the blessings of living for Jesus but also the impending judgment for those who rebel against God by rejecting His Son.

WRAP-UP

Before we end our time together, review what you've learned over the last seven sessions. Read through the key areas of emphasis on the following chart and record a brief answer to each question.

SESSION	REFLECTION QUESTION	YOUR ANSWER
Introducing Isaiah	How were hope and judgment both included in Isaiah's message?	
Trust God's Character	What character qualities or names for God have stood out to you from your study of Isaiah?	
Trust God's Calendar	How have you trusted the Lord's timing in your life over the course of the study?	
Trust God's Comfort	How have you experienced God's comfort in the pages of Isaiah?	
Trust God's Commands	How have you found peace in following God's instructions recently?	
Trust God's Correction	How have you experienced God's correction, and what benefits have you received from it?	
Trust God's Coming	What is one blessing Isaiah mentioned that you are looking forward to experiencing after Jesus returns?	

Session Seven
GROUP TIME

REVIEW
Use the following Scripture passages and questions to discuss what you learned in your personal Bible study.

Recall the Big Idea for each of the five days of study.

Read Isaiah 60:1-3. Discuss together your definitions for "the glory of the Lord" (p. 144) and brainstorm ways a person's life can bring God glory.

Share how you filled in the blank on page 149 to this sentence: Lord, Your will be done with _____. What connections have you made between trust and prayer?

Review the three key headings for Day Three: Complain to the Creator, Ask for Action, Recognize Roles (pp. 152-154). Share responses to the Daily Wrap-Up question on page 155.

Read Isaiah 65:17-25. Discuss your answers to the question, How does Isaiah's glimpse into the future encourage you spiritually (p. 158)?

Share your responses to this question on page 161: What have you discovered about striving less and trusting God more over the course of our study in the book of Isaiah?

MEMORIZE
Review Isaiah 64:4 and give the group an opportunity to recite it aloud.

WATCH

Use the fill-in-the-blanks and note-taking space as you watch the Session 7 teaching video together as a group.

We want to live in the _____ of His coming.

It's a relationship with Jesus that is the _____ and the _____ for all eternity (Isa. 60:1-3,19-20).

What to do while we wait for His return?

1._____ with God and others (Isa. 62:1; 64:1).

   Anything that drives you to prayer is a _____.

2._____ ourselves (Isa. 61:1-3).

3. _____ wholeheartedly our lives to Him
   (2 Pet. 3:11-14; 1 Thess. 5:23-24).

WOW: _____

WOE: _____

NOTES

PRAY

Close your time in prayer as a group. Thank God for the hope you have as we anticipate trust His future coming!

Leader Guide

LEADER TIPS

PRAY DILIGENTLY

Ask God to prepare you to lead this study. Pray individually and specifically for the girls in your group. Make this a priority in your personal walk and preparation.

PREPARE ADEQUATELY

Don't just wing this. Take time to preview each session so you have a good grasp of the content. Look over the group session and consider your students. Feel free to delete or reword the questions provided and add questions that fit your group better.

PROVIDE RESOURCES

Each girl will need a Bible study book. Try to have extras on hand for girls who join the group later in the study. Also suggest students bring a Bible and journal to group each week.

ENCOURAGE FREELY

Cheer for your girls and encourage them to participate in every part of the study.

LEAD BY EXAMPLE

Make sure you complete all of the personal study. Be willing to share your story, what you're learning, and your questions as you discuss together.

BE AWARE

If girls are hesitant to discuss their thoughts and questions in a larger group, consider forming smaller groups to provide a setting more conducive to conversation.

FOLLOW UP

If a girl mentions a prayer request or need, make sure to follow up. It may be a situation where you can get others in the group involved in helping out.

EVALUATE OFTEN.

After each session and throughout the study, assess what needs to be changed to more effectively lead the study.

MAKE THE MOST OF YOUR GROUP TIME

1. **Create a welcoming environment.** The space that your group is held doesn't have to be fancy, but what are you doing to make the girls feel safe and wanted each week? An easy way to do this is by starting off each group time with a snack or icebreaker game before jumping into review and discussion.

2. **Allow girls to wrestle with the Big Ideas.** As you encourage your girls to lean into discussion, help them know it's okay to ask hard questions and wrestle with new truths they are learning. The Big Ideas each week aren't always going to be easy to comprehend, but remind them that it's not about understanding fully; it's about trusting God fully.

3. **Connect with your girls before and after your group time.** Find a time each week to send a text to each girl (or in a group message) and ask them to share one thing they are learning and how they want to live it out. This will hold them accountable during their personal study days, and it will be such an encouragement for girls to hear what their peers are learning. (Oh, and we have weekly sharable graphics you can send them by scanning the QR code at the bottom of this page!)

4. **Take girls deeper in their knowledge and love of God's Word.** Lead the way in memorizing each session's Bible verse, and help your girls understand the importance of hiding God's Word in their hearts. Another way to encourage your girls to go deeper is to have them follow the Bible reading plan (p. 170) together as a group or in accountability pairs.

5. **Give girls ownership during the group times.** You might have one student lead the group discussion each week, while another student leads the prayer time. Make sure to prepare students ahead of time, but this will be so key in them leading out among their peers and owning their faith.

 Scan this QR code to access more leader resources + social assets!

Looking for the fill-in-the-blank answers for each session's Watch guide? Look on page 174.

Mom + Daughter Guide

HEY MOM!

We are so excited that you have decided to complete this study with your daughter. On these pages, Melissa Spoelstra guides you through the book of Isaiah by first looking at the significance of his prophecies in his own day before looking at their meaning for our lives today. In every session is an invitation for both you and your daughter to strive less and trust God more. You have a special opportunity to partner with your daughter on the path of learning to trust God above all and see every moment as grace.

YOU WILL NEED

Isaiah: Women's Bible Study Book for yourself

Isaiah: Teen Girl Bible Study Book for your daughter(s)

Isaiah: Teen Girl Video Sessions (additional purchase)

HOW TO USE YOUR MATERIALS TOGETHER

WATCH

Watch the weekly video with your daughter.

Use the questions found in Review at the beginning of each week's Group Time section located in the teen girl Bible study book.

A note about the video content: When studying together, you are welcome to watch the teen girls' or women's videos. The same content is covered in both versions, but the women's videos are between 20-30 minutes with a short discussion time. The teen videos include guided notes and may be shorter, depending on the session.

Please note that the fill-in-the-blanks found in the teen Bible study book are based on the teen videos. Those answers can be found on page 172.

As you both work through your individual Bible study books, you will discover that the teen girls' version might be slightly different as we altered some language and content to be more applicable for teen girls. However, there are very few differences in the studies and we encourage you to discuss what the Lord is teaching you individually.

CONNECT WITH HER

Plan days to work on personal study together to keep each other accountable.

Be open with your daughter throughout the week about things you learn or have questions about. Provide a safe place for her to do the same.

Don't stress! Some weeks will be easier than others to accomplish the personal study days. Just keep pressing forward and making it a priority to meet together each week regardless of how much personal study work was actually done.

FAQ

Q: How old does my teen need to be for this study?
A: *This study is recommended for girls ages 11 and up.*

Q: Are there other studies I can do with my daughter after this study is over?
A: *Yes! Many of our studies have both women's and teen girls' materials available. Check them out at lifeway.com/girls.*

READ THROUGH ISAIAH

SESSION ONE:
INTRODUCING ISAIAH

SESSION TWO: TRUST
GOD'S CHARACTER
☐ Day One: Isaiah 1; 2
☐ Day Two: Isaiah 3; 4
☐ Day Three: Isaiah 5; 6
☐ Day Four: Isaiah 7; 8; 9
☐ Day Five: Isaiah 10; 11; 12

SESSION THREE: TRUST
GOD'S CALENDAR
☐ Day One: Isaiah 13; 14
☐ Day Two: Isaiah 15; 16; 17
☐ Day Three: Isaiah 18; 19; 20
☐ Day Four: Isaiah 21; 22
☐ Day Five: Isaiah 23; 24

SESSION FOUR: TRUST
GOD'S COMFORT
☐ Day One: Isaiah 25; 26
☐ Day Two: Isaiah 27; 28
☐ Day Three: Isaiah 29; 30
☐ Day Four: Isaiah 31; 32; 33
☐ Day Five: Isaiah 34; 35

SESSION FIVE: TRUST
GOD'S COMMANDS
☐ Day One: Isaiah 36; 37
☐ Day Two: Isaiah 38; 39
☐ Day Three: Isaiah 40; 41
☐ Day Four: Isaiah 42; 43
☐ Day Five: Isaiah 44; 45; 46

SESSION SIX: TRUST
GOD'S CORRECTION
☐ Day One: Isaiah 47; 48
☐ Day Two: Isaiah 49; 50
☐ Day Three: Isaiah 51; 52
☐ Day Four: Isaiah 53; 54
☐ Day Five: Isaiah 55; 56

SESSION SEVEN: TRUST
GOD'S COMING
☐ Day One: Isaiah 57; 58
☐ Day Two: Isaiah 59; 60
☐ Day Three: Isaiah 61; 62
☐ Day Four: Isaiah 63; 64
☐ Day Five: Isaiah 65; 66

HOW TO BECOME A CHRISTIAN

Romans 10:17 says, "So faith comes from hearing, that is, hearing the Good News about Christ."

Maybe you've stumbled across new information in this study. Or maybe you've attended church all your life, but something you read here struck you differently than it ever has before. If you have never accepted Christ but would like to, read on to discover how you can become a Christian.

Your heart tends to run from God and rebel against Him. The Bible calls this sin. Romans 3:23 says, "For everyone has sinned; we all fall short of God's glorious standard."

Yet God loves you and wants to save you from sin, to offer you a new life of hope. John 10:10b says, "My purpose is to give them a rich and satisfying life."

To give you this gift of salvation, God made a way through His Son, Jesus Christ. Romans 5:8 says, "But God showed his great love for us by sending Christ to die for us while we were still sinners."

You receive this gift by faith alone. Ephesians 2:8-9 says, "God saved you by his grace when you believed. And you can't take credit for this; it is a gift from God. Salvation is not a reward for the good things we have done, so none of us can boast about it."

Faith is a decision of your heart demonstrated by the actions of your life. Romans 10:9 says, "If you openly declare that Jesus is Lord and believe in your heart that God raised him from the dead, you will be saved."

If you trust that Jesus died for your sins and want to receive new life through Him, pray a prayer similar to the following to express your repentance and faith in Him:

Dear God, I know I am a sinner. I believe Jesus died to forgive me of my sins. I accept Your offer of eternal life. Thank You for forgiving me of all my sins. Thank You for my new life. From this day forward, I will choose to follow You.

If you have trusted Jesus for salvation, please share your decision with your group leader or another Christian friend. If you are not already attending church, find one in which you can worship and grow in your faith. Following Christ's example, ask to be baptized as a public expression of your faith.

ENDNOTES

SESSION ONE

1. Warren W. Wiersbe, *Be Comforted: Feeling Secure in the Arms of God, Old Testament Commentary: Isaiah* (Colorado Springs, CO: David C. Cook, 2009), 125.
2. Ibid.
3. H. B. Charles Jr. "The Test of True Worship," Apr 8, 2019. Available online at https://hbcharlesjr.com.

SESSION TWO

1. John N. Oswalt, *Isaiah, The NIV Application Commentary* (Grand Rapids: Zondervan, 2003), 72.
2. Walter Bruggemann, *Isaiah 1-39* (Louisville: Westminster John Knox Press, 1998), 15.
3. Merrill F. Unger, *The New Unger's Bible Dictionary*, ed. R. K. Harrison, rev. and updated editions (Chicago: Moody Press, 1988), 1137.
4. Ibid., Gaebelein, 13.
5. Geoffrey W. Grogan, "Isaiah," *The Expositor's Bible Commentary: Proverbs–Isaiah, Revised Edition* (Grand Rapids, MI: Zondervan, 2008). Gaebelein, 55.
6. Ibid., Oswalt, 39.
7. "*Qadowsh*," Strong's: 6918. Accessed online at www.biblestudytools.com.
8. Kay Arthur, *Lord, I Want to Know You* (Colorado Springs: Waterbrook Press, 1992), 55. Also see "The Names of God in the Old Testament" online at www.bluletterbible.org/study/misc/name_god.cfm.
9. Ann Spangler, *The Names of God* (Grand Rapids: Zondervan, 2009), 35.
10. "*Elohim*," Strong's: H430. Accessed online at blueletterbible.org.
11. "*Yatsar*," Strong's: 3335. Accessed online at www.biblestudytools.com.
12. J. Alec Motyer, *Isaiah: An Introduction and Commentary, Tyndale Old Testament Commentaries, Vol. 20* (Downers Grove: Intervarsity Press, 1999), 87.
13. Ibid., Oswalt, 140.
14. Ibid., Goldingay, 67.
15. Ibid., Motyer, 99.
16. Ibid., Goldingay, 71.
17. Ibid., Motyer, 102.
18. Ibid., Oswalt, 146.

SESSION THREE

1. Sharon Rusten and E. Michael, *The Complete Book of When & Where in the Bible and throughout History* (Wheaton, IL: Tyndale House Publishers, Inc., 2005.)
2. Ibid., Wiersbe, 109; Ibid., Motyer, 249. See also https://enduringword.com/bible-commentary/2-kings-18/. Note: Co-regency among kings was a common practice during Isaiah's time. A king would partner with his son in leadership for many years before completely handing over the reins of leadership.
3. Ibid., Wiersbe, 109.
4. Ibid., Motyer, 249.
5. Ibid., Wiersbe, 110; Motyer, 249.
6. Ibid., Wiersbe, 109.
7. Ibid., Wiersbe, 118; Gaebelein, 236.
8. Ibid., Oswalt, 427.
9. Ibid., Wiersbe, 119.
10. Ibid., Oswalt, 422.
11. "*Miktab*," Strong's: 4385. Accessed online at www.biblestudytools.com. Ibid., Oswalt, 428.
12. "586 BC," Ibid., Rusten.
13. Ibid., Gaebelein, 239.
14. Brian Tracy, *Eat that Frog: 21 Great Ways to Stop Procrastinating and Get More Done in Less Time*, (Oakland: Berrett-Koehler Publishers, 2001), 22–23.
15. Ibid., Gaebelein, 274.
16. Ibid., Oswalt, 529.
17. Charles Boutell, *Haydn's Bible Dictionary* (New York: Ward, Lock & Co.: 1883), 67.
18. Ibid., Wiersbe, 144.
19. Ibid., 146.

SESSION FOUR

1. Ibid., Goldingay, 222.
2. Ibid., Gaebelein, 243.
3. Ibid., Motyer, 283.
4. "*Qavah*," Strong's: 6960. Accessed online at www.biblestudytools.com.
5. Trevor Haynes, "Dopamine, Smartphones & You: A battle for your time," Harvard Medical School Blog, May 1, 2018. Accessed online at https://sitn.hms.harvard.edu.
6. Ibid., Oswalt, 465.
7. Ibid., Oswalt, 460.
8. Ibid.
9. "*Towebah*," Strong's: 8441. Accessed online at www.biblestudytools.com.

10. Timothy Keller, *Counterfeit Gods: The Empty Promises of Money, Sex, and Power, and the Only Hope That Matters* (New York: Penguin, 2009), xvii.

11. "*Nacham,*" Strong's: 5162. Accessed online at www.biblestudytools.com.

12. Ibid., Gaebelein, 261.

13. Ibid., 264.

14. Brown, Driver, Briggs, and Gesenius, *The NAS Old Testament Hebrew Lexicon,* "Shuwb," Strong's: 7725. Accessed online at www.biblestudytools.com.

15. "*Ga'al,*" Strong's: 1350. Accessed online at www.biblestudytools.com.

16. Ibid., Oswalt, 470.

17. Ibid., Unger, 1069.

SESSION FIVE

1. Ibid, Oswalt, 538

2. "*Shama,*" Strong's: 8085. Accessed online at www.biblestudytools.com.

3. Isaiah 48 verses: 1,3,5,6,7,8,12,14,16,20

4. Motyer, 356.

5. "*Batach,*" Strong's: 982. Accessed online at www.biblestudytools.com.

6. "*Sha'an,*" Strong's: 8172. Accessed online at www.biblestudytools.com.

7. Ibid., Gaebelein, 186.

8. Ibid., Oswalt, 588

SESSION SIX

1. "*Mishpat,*" Strong's: 4941. Accessed online at www.biblestudytools.com.

2. Ibid., Oswalt, 472.

3. Ibid., 168.

4. C. S. Lewis, *Mere Christianity*, Book 3, Chapter 8, "The Great Sin," Kindle location 1665.

5. C. S. Lewis, *The Problem of Pain* (San Francisco: Harper Collins, 1940), 91.

6. Ibid., Gaebelein, 183.

7. Walter Bruggemann, *Isaiah 40-66* (Louisville: Westminster John Knox Press, 1998), 182.

8. Ibid., Motyer, 400.

9. "*Shalowm,*" Strong's: 7965. Accessed online at www.biblestudytools.com.

10. Ibid., Gaebelein, 88.

11. Ibid., Wiersbe, 50.

SESSION SEVEN

1. Ibid., Unger, 479.

2. Ibid., Wiersbe, 181.

3. Ibid., Oswalt, 641.

4. Ibid., 646.

5. Ibid., Gaebelein, 333.

6. Ibid., Motyer, 432.

7. Ibid., Unger, 1297.

8. "*Shamar,*" Strong's: 8104. Accessed online at www.biblestudytools.com.

9. Ibid., Gaebelein, 343.

10. Ibid., Wiersbe, 188.

11. Ibid., Wiersbe, 188; Ibid., Oswalt, 689.

12. Ibid., Oswalt, 689.

13. Charles Spurgeon, as quoted in Greg Morse, "Over Our Dead Bodies Embracing the Costs of Warning the Lost" desiringGod.org. Available online at www. desiringgod.org.

VIDEO VIEWER GUIDE ANSWERS

SESSION ONE

problem / tension
Never changing / ever changing
sovereign / surrendered
truth / timetable
comfort
heart / habits
heartache
His coming
afflicting / comforting

SESSION TWO

sovereign / surrendered
past / present
trust
holy / higher
Wow / Woe
good / authority
rituals / hearts
WOW: A vision of God reveals that He is our sovereign King.
WOE: We need clarity about God's character.

SESSION THREE

us / God
truth / timetable
Word of God / prayer
natural / supernatural
intervenes
prayer
threat / threatening
WOW: God's timing is perfect.

WOE: We need to trust God's timeline in our lives.

SESSION FOUR

weaken / strengthen
escape / distraction
comfort
get / go
counterfeits / true desire
idle / idols
shrink / level
association / Comforter
WOW: We serve a God who longs to comfort His people.
WOE: We have to stop turning to the counterfeit comforts.

SESSION FIVE

behavior
heart / habits
outside / inside
Lips / lives
align / fix
rebellion / listen
listening
His Word
depend
value / value
WOW: Jesus died for me.
WOE: Jesus called us to come and die to ourselves, to follow after Him.

SESSION SIX

correction
Scripture / Scripture
Love
Pride
Treatment / neglect
Father / snake
perfect
Jesus
WOW: God loves us enough to correct our course.
WOE: We welcome His warnings.

SESSION SEVEN

light
power / prize
Communicate
gift
Calm
Commit
WOW: Jesus is coming back.
WOE: We want to live differently in light of that truth.

Get the most from your study.

Customize your Bible study time with a guided experience.

In this study you'll:

- Learn to trust God for who He is and how He reveals Himself in Scripture
- Grow in understanding of the book of Isaiah and its prophecies
- Grasp how Jesus fulfills the promises in the book of Isaiah
- Discover peace in God's commands, character, and comfort

To enrich your study experience, consider the accompanying *Isaiah* video teaching sessions, approximately 25–30 minutes, from Melissa Spoelstra. To purchase access to these videos, visit lifeway.com/isaiah.

Looking for more resources for teen girls? Visit lifeway.com/girls to shop our latest Bible studies and devotionals.